FIRST GENERATION FATHER

FIRST GENERATION FATHER

How to Build a Healthy and Happy Home When You Come From a Broken One

ANTHONY BLANKENSHIP

**EVERYTHING
CONNECTS
MEDIA**

FIRST GENERATION FATHER
*How to Build a Healthy and Happy Home
When You Come From a Broken One*

ISBN   978-1-5445-1603-5 *Hardcover*
       978-1-5445-1602-8 *Paperback*
       978-1-5445-1601-1 *Ebook*
       978-1-5445-1649-3 *Audiobook*

To Sarah, Adrian, and Cassidy.
Thank you for making me a better man.

CONTENTS

PROLOGUE

WORST TYPE OF SOLDIER

Early during my basic training (commonly referred to as boot camp), our drill sergeants had us grab some specific gear and hustle into formation outside the barracks. In basic training, everything happens at a hurried pace. If you do anything casually, you're asking to get "smoked"—which means exercised to exhaustion as a form of punishment. I quickly learned to pay attention to instructions the first time they were given. And to always move with a sense of purpose. We grabbed our newly acquired gear and scrambled to the drill pad.

As we stood there awaiting instructions, I had the feeling this was a smoke trap. That's a situation designed for us to fail so the drill sergeants could work the hell out of us. Which they seemed to enjoy doing. If you're not familiar with military training, this may sound unfair or cruel. Trust me, it's both. But it also serves an important purpose. Facing almost impossible tasks in stressful situations, with physical consequences should you fail, is exactly the type of training combat soldiers should endure. Besides, it's just exercise.

We stood in silence, eyes front. I hugged my bulky bag of unfamiliar gear and waited for my next command. As the minutes crawled by, the bag grew heavier and tougher to hang on to. A slow burn worked its way from my forearms up into my shoulders. I refused to let myself imagine the relief of setting it down. I dug my fingers into it until they were numb. I had a flashback to this bulging bag I carried for years during my childhood paper route. Your mind makes lots of weird connections during stressful situations. The drill sergeants moved through our ranks in a stealthy silence. They were like sharks under the surface of calm water, waiting for a toe to dangle over the edge of a boat and then...*chomp!* We held on for dear life. But eventually, the inevitable happened.

Clang, cla-clang, clang! Someone dropped their metal canteen cup. The sound punched a hole in the silence. I gasped internally. I think we all did. It reminded me of a cartoon when someone is hiding behind a curtain to avoid a monster, and just before the monster leaves the room...*achoo!* The drill sergeants' heads snapped up in unison. A toe was in the water, and there was about to be a feeding frenzy.

The U.S. Army taught me some of the most valuable life lessons I've ever learned. I spent a total of five years on active duty service—two years as an enlisted soldier and three years as a commissioned officer. In that time, I had some life-changing experiences, including spending a year in Korea and a year in Iraq. No matter where the army landed me, each place was packed with significant learning opportunities. One of the most valuable lessons I took from the military—one that I use every single day as a husband and father—is this: leadership is service.

I was fortunate enough to serve under, and alongside, some

remarkable people. True warriors with the highest of characters. I watched the leaders I respected the most. I incorporated elements of their leadership style into my own. As an officer, I outranked many soldiers. But rank doesn't equal leadership. My goal was to serve the soldiers in my unit and to earn their respect. Not by outranking them but by being a good leader for them.

What I didn't know is the fundamental principle I was using to lead soldiers—leadership is service—would one day be the same fundamental principle I'd use to build a healthy and happy family. I hadn't yet learned that everything connects, but I soon would. In a way, the seed for this book was planted during an army experience. One that all service members are familiar with, getting my ass chewed by a drill sergeant at basic training.

Drill sergeants are the stuff of legend. The very best of them are part instructor, part psychologist, and part comedian. Their observation skills are unmatched. Nothing slips past them. They motivate young soldiers with a wide variety of tools that span from sincere encouragement on one end of the spectrum, all the way to a profanity-laced roasting on the other end. Either way, you're also doing push-ups. Some of the funniest stuff I've ever heard in my life came while I was drenched in sweat, muscles shaking from fatigue, listening to a drill sergeant verbally annihilate somebody. The fact that we weren't supposed to laugh only made it that much funnier.

That morning, when the canteen cup clanged onto the pavement, I knew things were about to get ugly. I tried to keep my mind off the pain in my arms by focusing on my surroundings. I noticed that, against a wall, there were three bags just like the ones we were holding. The outside of each bag was organized in a very particular way. Dress-right-dress, meaning each one matched the others perfectly. Ruck suck with a pistol belt around the base, two canteen cup holders evenly spaced from the center, road guard vest over the closed ruck, PT mat on top, everything in its place. I knew those bags must belong to the drill sergeants. In my mind, I started organizing the contents of my bag so that it matched theirs—canteens here, road guard vest there, PT mat across the top, etc. I took note of as much detail as I could. Anything to keep my mind off the poor guy who had dropped his canteen cup. The drill sergeants were letting him have it.

Once the frenzy calmed down, a drill sergeant grabbed one of the bags I had just been looking at. He held it up for us all to see, and then he shouted what he surely thought was an impossible task: "Alright! You've got one minute to make your gear look like this gear. Go!"

There was an immediate crash as exhausted arms gave out all around me. Followed by panicked confusion. "A minute to do what?" someone whispered. "Make it look like what?" someone else asked. But I had already completed the task several times in my mind while the drill sergeants were occupied with the poor soul behind me. I couldn't believe my luck. I was semiconfident I could actually pull this off.

Instead of dumping my gear everywhere, I set it down quickly but gently. Then I started flying through the task. *Belt, flashlight, magazine holders...*

I could hear some guys around me bickering, "Hey, those are mine!" There was no way they were gonna make it. Guaranteed chum. But I was locked in. I glanced up every so often at the drill sergeants' reference bags. But by the time they started their countdown at "TEN SECONDS!" I was already done. My bag wasn't perfect, but it was in the ballpark. And it was leaps and bounds ahead of anyone else. I stood at attention behind my display. Proud. Silent. Perfectly still. The rest of the group scrambled around me as the drill sergeant finished his countdown, "...3...2...1...Freeze!"

Everyone stopped and stood behind their sloppy piles, frustration on their faces. But I held my chin high in victory. My bag sat neatly organized, alone in a sea of chaos. The drill sergeants looked at us disapprovingly. I didn't realize it, but they disapproved of one soldier more than the others. That soldier was me.

From the corner of my eye I could see one drill sergeant nudge another and nod his head in my direction. I had obviously stood out. When one of them started walking my way, I assumed he was coming over to congratulate me. I was actually that clueless. Just before he got to me, though, he stopped. There was a moment of uncertain tension, then he reared his boot back. Only then did it dawn on me, *I don't think he's here to congratulate me.*

It was as if he summoned the rage and fury of every drill sergeant that ever lived, and channeled it into one thunderous kick. *BOOM!* His boot caught my bag perfectly square. He leaned into it with every molecule of his being. My neat little display exploded like a party popper. And my bag's contents rained down on the drill pad like confetti.

In an instant I went from confused to defensive. I figured

they were upset I'd beat them at their own game. Like I said, I was clueless. Fortunately, my drill sergeant was about to enlighten me.

He leaned into me real close. Uncomfortably close. So close I could feel his breath against my ear. I braced myself to be screamed at. But instead, he whispered. This message wasn't for everybody. It was just for me. His words changed my perspective forever and eventually led to this book.

He said, "You're the worst type of soldier."

I kept my military bearing, eyes front, unmoving. He repeated himself. This time even more sure of it, "Yeah, you're the *worst* type of soldier." I blinked.

"Look around," he said. "Look."

I broke my stare and looked around. The drill pad was a mess. Loose gear was sprawled everywhere. I sensed there was a connection to be made, but I struggled to see it.

"Your fellow soldiers could have used some help," he said. "And you had help to give. But all you cared about was you." I looked down at what remained of my once neat display and felt ashamed. I had a lot to learn.

A SOLDIER WHO GREW FROM MISTAKES

While doing the push-ups that came with this lesson, I had a revelation: every challenge we face is about more than the challenge itself. The challenge is just a tool, a mechanism for us to meet ourselves at newer, deeper levels. Success then comes from reflecting on what we discover and making the necessary changes to grow and evolve. This is as true in everyday life as it is in basic training.

As a first generation father, it's *especially* true. There are going to be plenty of things you get wrong, and that's OK. As long as you're willing to reflect and commit to the changes necessary to grow and evolve, you're succeeding.

You and I are both soldiers fighting the same fight. We're trying to overcome the effects of a broken home, of unhealthy family situations. We're trying to face, and heal from, certain traumatic events from our past. We're trying to be the husbands our wives deserve, and the leaders our children need. Our mission is to create something better for our loved ones than we had ourselves. This starts with making something better *of ourselves*. As you'll hear me say from time to time in this book, everything connects.

In the army, soldiers are assigned to groups called units. I've seen some units do amazing things, and I've seen others fail miserably. In my experience, units don't fail because their people are incapable. Units fail because their people are selfish, because they don't care about one another. But when everyone in a unit puts the person next to him *ahead* of himself, that unit is unbreakable. This same principle holds true for a family. As the husband and father in your household, this starts with you.

By no means do I claim to know it all. There is no arriving at being a great father and husband. It's a continual journey, an ongoing process of learning and growing. But in my twenty-plus years of loving my wife, I've learned a few things. I've made a few connections. And by some miracle, my bag is in order.

As you set out on your mission to build a healthy and happy home, know that you are not alone. There are scores of us, fighting our own fights, trying to find a way to do what once seemed impossible—committed to the mission of being a first generation father. I'm proud to be a part of your journey, even if it's in the smallest way.

Now strap up, and let's roll. Your family is depending on you.

INTRODUCTION

WHAT IS A FIRST GENERATION FATHER?

A first generation father is any man who grew up without a positive example of what a father should be—and is now trying to figure it out for himself. It's any man working to break the cycle of dysfunction he came from, and provide better for his own family. That said, being a first generation father isn't just about raising children. It's also about identifying toxic relationship patterns you've come to see as normal and replacing them with healthy ones. It's about doing the deeply personal work of healing, growing, and balancing.

This is difficult to do. It's hard to build the type of love where both people feel fulfilled and content. It's hard to create an environment where children are safe from physical and emotional trauma, and are raised to see the world as a loving place. It's hard to find financial stability and a healthy balance of abundance and appreciation. Homes where these things are the norm are hard to build, and they're even harder to maintain. If you come from dysfunction, drama, and scars—homes like this may seem to only exist in fairy tales.

What defines a broken home? For our purposes, there is no singular definition. Maybe your parents went through a tough divorce. Maybe they were never married, like mine. Maybe one of them had addiction issues, or anger issues, or infidelity issues. Maybe one of them was abusive or neglectful. Maybe there was no real "trauma" in your home, but your emotional needs weren't met. Maybe your parents stayed together in a loveless, resentful marriage. There are so many ways homes can be broken. No matter what your situation was, if you want to do better for your family, this book will help you.

MY QUALIFICATIONS

You may be wondering what my qualifications are to talk about these things. Well, I'm a first generation father myself. I was born to a teenaged high school dropout. She was a single parent, and we had no place to live. Things started off tough, and got worse before they got better. Much worse. I was exposed to violence, poverty, drug abuse, manipulative relationships, and more. This was my normal. And the dysfunction left plenty of scars.

My own father has seven children with five different women. Meaning I have siblings from four different mothers. Like I said, there are lots of ways for families to be broken. Eventually, my father did ten years in prison. This made one thing clear to me: if I was gonna break the cycle and become more than just a product of my environment, I was gonna have to figure out how to do it on my own. And I did.

Today, I'm a happily married father of two. I've been with my beautiful and talented wife, Sarah, for more than twenty years now. In that time, I've had to do a lot of growing, learning, and evolving. In this book, I'll give you the most valuable lessons I've learned on my journey. I'll give you the exact tools and understanding that I used to build and maintain my healthy and happy home. And I'll present them in a way that's easy to understand and allows you to apply them to your own life.

OTHERS ARE WELCOME

I welcome all readers. In fact, I wrote this book hoping the truths in it would resonate with a broad base. Although the language I use may sound specific to fathers, the principles and teachings are applicable to everyone. The benefits of recognizing and healing old wounds, mastering our three primal energies, and ascending to the highest versions of ourselves are universal. They are just as applicable for women as they are for men. There are plenty of first generation mothers out there trying to break negative family cycles too.

If you're a stepfather, or you're in a serious relationship with a woman who has a child, please read this book. What's in it will help you better understand yourself, and better understand how to lead—be of service to—your family. This is the last time I'll make a distinction between stepfather and biological father. If you're the adult male in a child's life, take these teachings and apply them.

If you're a woman who's in love with a first generation father, I encourage you to read this book too. It'll give you some insight into the challenges he faces. Together, the two of you can help each other heal, find your balance, and move to new depths of genuine love in your relationship.

Same goes for my LGBTQ friends. Many of you have suffered

painful traumas in your life that may still be hurting you and negatively affecting your relationships today. I believe the lessons in this book will help you on your journey to healing and self-actualization. The techniques I share of dealing with past pain to ensure you don't subconsciously pass it on to your own children are critical. Welcome.

WHAT THIS BOOK IS

First Generation Father is a treasure map. Follow it, and you'll successfully navigate the traps of confusion and frustration that have cost so many well-meaning people their families. It'll lead you directly into the golden zone of a healthy and happy relationship based on mutual love and respect for each other. And it'll help you find the balance you need in order to provide physically, mentally, and emotionally for your loved ones. This book will be funny sometimes. It'll be serious sometimes. And it'll be honest all the time.

I don't claim to know it all. In a lot of ways, I'm still growing as a husband and as a father. But if you read this book with an open heart and an open mind, you'll put it down a better person than you were when you picked it up.

While we're on the topic, here are a few things this book is not. It's not political. These days, it seems as if everything is politicized. But broken homes and damaged families affect people of all political affiliations. The messages and techniques in this book are valid and applicable for you despite your social, political, or religious beliefs.

This book is also not racially exclusive. First generation fathers exist in every race and ethnicity. The principles don't change.

We are all brothers of a shared experience. Soldiers with the same mission: to overcome our pasts, and ourselves, so that we can do what's best for our families.

Lastly, this book is not a tell-all. I am not here to air out anyone in my life's dirty laundry. In fact, some of the most salacious parts of my early life story, parts that left profound and lasting scars, have been intentionally left out. I do share quite a bit of my personal history on the forthcoming pages. But only to give my journey of becoming a first generation father the proper context. This book will ask you to evaluate some painful experiences from your past. And I couldn't ask you to look at your own pain without being willing to show you some of mine.

LET'S DO IT

I hope you enjoy *First Generation Father*. It took the first forty-three years of my life to learn these lessons and organize them for you. It's been a long haul. But if this book helps you accomplish your mission—and establish a healthy and happy home for your family—it will have been worth it. I respect the hell out of what you're trying to do, and I'm proud to be a part of it. Remember, leading your family means serving your family. In order to serve your family, you need to be healthy and balanced yourself. So we'll start there. This won't be easy. But accomplishing great things never is. I believe in you. You got this. Let's do it.

CHAPTER 1

• • •

SCARS: FACING THE PAIN FROM YOUR PAST

Before I tell you about the time my father sank a lit match into my face, I wanna tell you about a certain human reaction to injury called the reflex arc. Have you ever been burned? It's a terrible pain, but your body has an interesting reaction to it. If you were to touch a hot pan, you would instinctively yank your hand away without thinking about it. Your brain would bypass regular communication pathways, and your body would just react. That little trick is called the reflex arc. It's part of our body's brilliant design to keep us safe and alive.

Later, after you're out of immediate danger, you have time to process what happened. That's when you fully feel the pain. And fully feeling the pain is important. That's where the lesson lies. That's when our mind makes the connection—*hot pans are dangerous. I need to be careful around them. My life may depend on it.* I was an adult when I learned about the reflex arc, but it jarred an early memory I have of my father.

I was five years old. My mom sent me to stay with him for a

weekend. He had a drug problem and a violence problem. He used to beat my mother, even while she was pregnant with me. Once, he beat her so bad she was hospitalized. Still, on this night, I found myself alone with him.

I'm not sure what he was smoking, but his eyes were a Devil shade of red. He smiled at me and lit a match. I can still hear that distinct striking sound, crisp and sharp. I can still smell the burning sulfur, still see the orange-and-blue flame dancing in its duality.

I use the word duality here because fire has the ability to destroy, but it also has the ability to purify. For all the damage it can cause, it can also cleanse, making a thing free from impurities.

We sat alone in the dark house. The TV was the only light. It caused schizophrenic color flashes to streak across the walls. Commercials blared advertisements, selling happiness and fun over cheesy '80s jingles. But I was not having fun. My stomach was in a knot. I felt nervous. I felt scared. I felt normal.

He sat shirtless on the couch. He watched the TV, but I watched him. When the screen cut to black, the darkness swallowed him. In an instant he was gone. The Devil had him now, a dragon of some sort, I was sure of it. And I suspected that one day it would come for me too. Then, just like that, the television would light up with colors, song, and canned laughter. He'd be back from the underworld. Eyes glassy. Off-balance. Every time the room went dark, I thought he was gone for good. And every time he came back, he was a little less of himself. He sat and stared ahead. Then he lit another match and turned his gaze at me.

The fire danced as he moved it toward me. Duality. How would its energy be used, to build or destroy? One flame, two very different outcomes. Such is the relationship between you and your scars. We all have them. We've all been burned one way or another. The question is, are you going to let your scars limit you? Are you going to pass your pain down to your own children? Or are you going to turn those scars into a source of strength, and let them serve you and your family? They can build or destroy; the choice is yours.

My father was dangerously out of balance. It's impossible to lead like that, to serve like that. All you can do when you're out of balance is hurt people—either yourself or others. His scars were getting the best of him. He'd chased a dragon into the darkness, and that dragon was burning him alive. Now, he reached out to me, with fire in his hand—about to make his scars mine.

As the distance between he and I lessened, the flame grew more intense. Until there was no more distance between us. His giant hand sank the lit match into the center of my fleshy cheek. It melted into me with ease. Before I could think, I yanked away—*reflex arc*. Now I know. After that came the pain. It was excruciating. It was a white-hot snakebite piercing my skin. Planting, in the middle of my face, for me to see forever, a lesson—a scar. A reminder of where I come from, and of the darkness awaiting me if I didn't figure out how to heal, evolve, and find balance.

The next day I went back home. The wound on my cheek was scabby and bloody. My father told my mother it was an accident. And that was that. Maybe it was an accident. Who can say for sure? But the fact is, that night has remained with me ever since. Over the years, the scar has faded. Most people barely notice it. But I've internalized it. It's become a part of who I am, and a source of strength that I use to serve me as a husband and as a father.

Trauma from our past still affects us today, especially as parents and spouses.

We all want to be good fathers. But many of us fail. We fail our children, we fail our partners, we fail ourselves. The question is, *why?* Why do we fail at something we care so deeply about? Oftentimes the answer is: our scars.

Scars are the leftover damage from traumas and injuries we've suffered. They can be physical, mental, or emotional. These scars can be dangerous to our mental health and well-being, and flat-out devastating to our ability to raise healthy and happy families.

Life scars all of us to some degree. Nobody gets out of this thing unscathed. The key to becoming strong men, loving husbands, and great fathers is learning to use our scars to make us stronger, rather than allowing them to make us weaker. Many of life's most valuable lessons come from pain and struggle. Therefore, our scars can be our biggest teachers. They can make us better people. But before that can happen, we need to treat our unhealed wounds. If we don't, they *will* become infected. And those infections will negatively impact your entire family. Keep reading, and I'll explain exactly how you can overcome your past injuries and use them to fuel your personal growth and development. This is something I learned how to do out of necessity because I was born accumulating scar tissue.

BORN A SHAME

As a kid, I used to cringe when someone would ask me, "Are your mom and dad still married?" I hated that question because they were never married. Keep in mind, this was middle America, Ohio, in 1977. There was a negative social stigma that came with being born out of wedlock. Labels were given to both my mother and me. None of them flattering. Society still has a way of shaming single mothers, but it was even worse back then.

Although I learned the definition of "bastard" at a cruelly young age, the real crown of shame placed on my head was about my race. I'm biracial, or as some folks say—mixed. This simply means, of two races. In my case: my mother is White, and my father is Black. Back then, people really didn't approve of mixed race kids. Hell, plenty of people don't approve of the idea now. But, don't worry, if my mixed race offends you or your sensibilities, let me just say...*it wasn't my idea! Nobody consulted me.*

I grew up Black and White in America. That's such a heavy thing to deal with. Think about it for a second. Black and White, IN AMERICA. You know what that means? It means that if you traced my ancestry back far enough, at one point in American history, I'd actually own myself. Shit is confusing.

OK, I know I said I wasn't going to divide this book down racial lines. And I'm not, I promise. But dammit, I've had to work through some trauma. So I've earned the right to joke around a bit! It's OK to laugh. We're gonna work our way through some serious stuff. The only way we're gonna make it is if we bring a sense of humor with us.

That said, you know who WASN'T laughing when his teenaged daughter turned up pregnant by a Black man? My grandfather. He was very old-fashioned. Very proud. Very White. He was born and raised in rural Tennessee, near the birthplace of the KKK. When he learned that his first grandson was gonna be my little illegitimate ass, no...he wasn't laughing. In fact, he kicked my mom out. Pregnant and all.

My mom had been a good student. But, given the severity of her life situation, school was no longer a priority. Predictably, she dropped out. My father was older and had finished school a few years before her. He didn't graduate either, he was just finished.

Today, there are all sorts of studies that show a direct correlation between the education and social status of parents, and how likely their child is to succeed in life. Educated parents raise educated children. Parents with high-earning careers are more likely to raise children with high-earning careers. It makes sense, really. People tend to become what they regularly see, especially children. Instinctively, we already know this. It's one of the reasons we want to do right by our own families, so that our children have a healthy and well-balanced sense of what is normal.

The normal I saw early was neither healthy nor balanced. Not only did my father have seven children with five different women, but he was also incredibly violent toward them. Many nights the sobs and screams of my mom bled through the walls of whatever room I was tucked in, and hung over my head like the Boogey Man. Threatening to eat me whole. Tears glued my eyes shut. A lump of tension ached in my throat. I'd need to pee, but I didn't dare leave the room. If I peed the bed, so be it. Better than facing what was happening on the other side of that door.

There's a very distinct energy in the air when you're around that type of thing, especially as a small child. Life feels dangerous. No one can be trusted. The people you instinctively look to for protection from danger, are the danger. It turns everything upside down from its natural order. It's a real mind fuck, and a lot of kids never recover from it. Many eventually become abusers themselves.

Late in my mom's pregnancy, my father beat her so bad she was hospitalized. While consulting with her for this part of the book, she admitted she thought I might die in her belly. I didn't have the nerve to ask her if she'd wanted me to. Life is great now, and she's been Grandma of the Year for like a decade straight. So, I'm sure she'd say no. But back then, she was a White teenaged, high school dropout in an abusive, drug-fueled relationship about to give birth to an unwelcomed, little Black boy. Me dying might have been easier on everybody. Her life was hard and only about to get harder. As for me, I hadn't even taken my first breath yet and was already disowned from one side of the family, and getting my ass kicked by the other. If pain fueled growth, I was gonna be a fucking giant.

MY DAYS AS JEFFREY

Luckily, I survived that early beating and lived through birth. Ironically, I was born on my father's birthday. I know, trippy, right? Although I had made it into the world, I wasn't welcomed with a sparkly banner that read, "It's a Boy!" I wasn't greeted by eager family ready to take me home and show me off to the world. I didn't have a home to go to at all. My mom didn't have a place for us to live. My dad wasn't really an option. And my grandfather refused to look at me, let alone allow us to live with him. So, my mom did what she felt she had to do. She gave me over to foster care.

She left me at a facility run by nuns. Although I'm not Catholic, those nuns kept me from being tossed into a dumpster somewhere, so they were doin' God's work in my book. This place wouldn't be my final destination. It was just a layover until I got plugged in with a longer-term foster family. These foster families would agree to keep kids for a certain period of time, while the birth parents got their feet under them.

Bein' the little light-skinned charmer that I was, I got swooped up by a family pretty quick. All of a sudden, I had a nice, safe place to stay. Life was lookin' up. But that safety came at a cost. My foster family didn't like the name Anthony, so they changed it. They renamed me Jeffrey. *Jeffrey*. No offense if that's your name, but I don't imagine myself ever giving off a "Jeffrey" vibe. But hey, when your other option is the dumpster behind Burger King, Jeffrey kinda has a nice ring to it.

My mom was busy trying to get things situated and safe enough for us both to live. During that time, she'd meet with my foster care caseworker every so often for progress reports. The lady would give her updates:

"Oh, *Jeffrey* is doing this. *Jeffrey* is doing that. *Jeffrey* cries a lot!"

My foster family thought I cried because of the type of formula I was getting. They said I had colic. But I believe I was just pissed they changed my name.

Foster mom: "Who's a hungry baby? Is *Jeffrey* a hungry baby? Oh, Jeff-wee is a hung-wee baby!"

Baby me: "Waaaaah! *Me*, lady! *I'm* hungry! Where's my momma!? And who the hell is Jeffrey!?"

God bless that family who took me in. They very well may have saved my life. After a few months in foster custody, my mom had herself together enough to come and take me back. She also gave me back my name. My days as Jeffrey were short, but they were indicative of my life to come—one faced with challenges, obstacles, and miraculous help when I needed it most.

THE SHARPEST WORDS

Children are beautifully honest. They don't worry about who they embarrass or offend. They just tell the unfiltered truth as they see it. It's sweet and innocent, but it can also be scary. Kind of like a toddler waddling around with a loaded gun. Kids fire off rounds of honesty with no warning shots. Unaware that nothing hurts people quite like the truth.

After some very rough years of us bouncing around and being in dangerous situations, my grandfather allowed my mom and I to move back into his house. He was evolving, for his family's sake. What a breakthrough. There was still tension, but at least we were safe.

One night my mom went to a house party. With nobody to babysit, she brought me with her. I was around seven years old. The party was jumpin'! Music, laughter, and marijuana smoke filled the air. I was familiar with the smell. I remember liking it right away.

I was the only kid there and I liked that too. It meant I got to watch and listen to the adults without being shooed away to play with someone else. I sat quietly and took in the show. Eventually, my eyes got too heavy, and I drifted off to sleep on the couch.

When I woke up, the party was over. The house felt strange now that it was dark and quiet. A streetlight cast an eerie yellowish glow through the window. I wasn't sure where my mom was. Had she left me here?

I noticed a blanket on the floor. Large and odd-shaped. It was moving. Then, from under it, I heard two hushed voices. One was a man, the other was a woman. My mom. Their whispered words became sounds—terrible grunts, moans, and hisses. Sounds that I couldn't unhear. My stomach ached its familiar, uneasy ache. I didn't understand what was happening, and I didn't want to. I just wanted it to stop.

Eventually, it did. I heard one of them get up. I pried open the corner of my eye and saw the man walking into the bathroom. He was naked. I tried my best to swallow the knot in my throat and squeezed my eyes shut until the sun came up.

The next day, we were back at my grandpa's house. He and my mom were talking in the kitchen. She was explaining why we hadn't come home last night. She told him she had fallen asleep. He seemed less than impressed with her explanation. I kept waiting for her to tell him about the man under the blanket, but she never did. In my attempt to add some clarity to the situation, I walked into the room, cocked my truth gun, and fired.

"I saw you with a naked man."

Looking back, it's funny how kids can be so oblivious to what's happening in a room. If I had been paying closer attention, I'd have noticed they were speaking in heated tones. If I had been able to see the bigger picture, I'd have noticed there were power struggle issues at play. But I was just a kid and didn't notice any of that...until it was too late. *I saw you with a naked man.* This was definitely gonna leave a scar.

Mom and Grandpa both froze, then each turned to look at me. I stood there, partly ignorant of what I'd just done, partly wanting to cut the shit. I knew what I saw. And I knew I was telling the truth. My grandpa walked away without another word.

This left my mom and I alone. Her eyes grew narrow and pointed as she glared at me. I didn't quite recognize her facial expression. I wasn't sure what it meant. Then, she spoke, and removed all doubt. She said, "I wish you were never born."

The words gathered themselves in a dark cloud over my head. I processed their meaning in silence. Then they rained down on me like acid. For years, I've scrubbed at them, trying to stop their burn. But as I've matured into adulthood, and became a parent myself, the thought of saying that to a child seems even more fucked-up now than it did then. *I wish you were never born.* Damn.

My mom has done a ton for me. I once heard her describe our relationship by saying, "We grew up together." Now that I have my own family, and I see how difficult it is, I can't imagine the stress and struggle she must have experienced raising me. She did the absolute best she could, given the situation. But scars don't go away. As parents, it's critical that we understand this. When we scar our children, we negatively impact the way they see the world and themselves. It may take a child a lifetime to fully recover from the crippling effects of our words and actions as a parent. That's if they're lucky enough to ever recover at all.

YOUR PAIN IS VALID

It's important for you to understand that your pain is valid. Your scars—the pain you've experienced in your life—whatever its source, is valid. It's real. Please don't fall into the trap of thinking that because your trauma wasn't "as bad" as someone else's, that you have no right to feel pain. This is how wounds go untreated and are left unhealed. We've all been exposed to different incidents of trauma and dysfunction; all of them are valid.

Not only is it OK for you to acknowledge how you've been hurt, but acknowledging your pain is the only way you'll ever truly get past it. If you don't, it'll haunt you forever. And worst of all, there's a good chance you'll pass that pain down to your child.

How terribly ironic is that? You deny your pain so that it doesn't affect you, but it ends up defining you when you pass it along to your own children. Don't allow that to happen. Heal yourself, and break the tragic—yet all too common—cycle of fathers passing down their unresolved issues as problems their children have to solve.

When you accept that your pain is real, you don't need it validated by anyone else. For many of us, our pain was denied by the very people who hurt us. A lot of first generation fathers, and adults in general, get stuck here. We never heal from the pain and trauma of our childhood because we're waiting for our parents to acknowledge and accept their responsibility in it. We're waiting for them to have a developmental breakthrough where they realize just how much stress and negativity some of their decisions put us through. But a lot of times, that never happens. Instead, these parents try to minimize and downplay the trauma and toxicity they exposed you to. They'll say things like, "Lots of kids had it worse." Or, "You always had a roof over your head." Be cautious of anyone who denies you the truth of your own feelings. It's a form of manipulative gaslighting.

While it's natural to want your pain validated by the person who hurt you, you can't tie your ability to heal to them accepting their role in your pain. If you do, you're giving away all of your power. Don't let them dictate your recovery. You need to heal because your family needs you healed. You need to be well because your family needs you well. You've got to ascend to a balanced place within yourself. And you can't let anyone prevent you from getting there.

It's quite common for the parents who raised you in trauma and drama to now try to rewrite history. To deny, deflect, and justify their actions—and how those actions hurt you. That can't matter anymore. Your healing can't be contingent upon your parents, or anyone else who may have caused you pain. If it is, you'll be hurting for the rest of your life.

FIGHT OR DIE

By the time I was twelve, I was fully aware that the world was a hostile place. I'd seen violence, drug abuse, and faced a fair share of racial discrimination. Sometimes folks assume that because I'm mixed, I've never really dealt with discrimination.

But that's backward—I've actually faced double discrimination! I've been hated on by White people and by Black people! I've been called a cracker *and* a nigger...by my own family! I've even been called a spic, and I'm not even Hispanic! I was like, "C'mon, Grandpa. I'm just eating a taco. This is getting ridiculous."

My mom and I had moved out of my grandpa's house and were now living in an apartment. Her boyfriend lived with us too. On more than one occasion, he rummaged through my room and stole whatever money I had to buy himself drugs. One year I shoveled snow all winter long. I saved every dollar. I was gonna buy a nice new bike in the spring. I had one already, but the thing felt like it weighed a hundred pounds. I was saving up to buy somethin' *dope*—like a Mongoose or a Dyno. That's what the coolest kids rode. But it never happened. Before spring rolled around, he found my newest hiding spot and cleaned me out. Stole every dollar. Losing that money hurt, but at least it didn't come with the indignity of getting beat up too.

In my next effort to get some money, I took a job as a paperboy for the *Toledo Blade*. I delivered papers to people's houses seven days a week. It was a hard job, but I liked the responsibility. Every day I'd fill my giant cloth sack with newspapers until the sides bulged. Then I'd lumber around the neighborhood with the bag hanging from my neck like a yoke. My route covered a pretty broad area, and the Ohio winters made it hell.

On collection day, I'd carry a Crown Royal bag with me. You know, the purple velvet ones. I'd put all the money in there for safekeeping. One day, as I was making my collections, a bigger, aggressive kid swore at me, knocked me down, and took it from me. I was so scared and unsure of what to do that I barely resisted. I didn't like violence. I'd seen people seriously hurt, and I didn't like the idea of hurting someone myself. I didn't want to fight. I wanted to go to school and get good grades and become a lawyer, which was always my dream. But on that long walk home, I started to feel different. I started to feel angry. I started to feel like the world was gonna make me fight, whether I wanted to or not. I felt ashamed that I didn't fight back harder, and upset that I even had to. As I walked, I replayed the incident in my mind over and over. Each time, I fought back more and more against the boy who robbed me. By the time I got home, in my mind, I'd killed him.

BY EXTENSION

I rarely saw my father these days. He'd married one of the women he dated while he was also dating my mom. The two women had a long and complicated history together. I'd seen and heard my dad beat both of them. Eventually my mom got away, and the other woman stayed. Now they were married.

One weekend, I found myself visiting my dad and his wife. He was out, and she was in charge of watching me and my brother (from another mother). My resentment toward the world had been brewing for some time. I was getting tired of being the good kid and having nothing but pain to show for it. I was done being pushed around, and done holding my tongue about things.

I made a detailed case to my dad's wife about why he was a terrible father, and a bad person in general. She listened intently and let me talk. I thought I was winning her over. After all, she'd been on the receiving end of so many ass whoopin's at my father's hands, I figured surely, she'd side with me. I was wrong. Years later, I read the autobiography of Frederick Douglass. And when I did, what happened at my father's that weekend made a lot more sense.

Frederick Douglass is an American legend. He was born a slave, endured heartbreaking hardships, taught himself to read, escaped to the North, and eventually ascended to become a presidential consultant on the Emancipation Proclamation and postslavery America. There's another special point of interest I have in Frederick Douglass—like me, he was mixed.

In his autobiography, he explained that his White father was a slave master, and his Black mother was a slave. This was an ugly commonality during that time. Masters would rape and impregnate their slaves. When the baby was born, the masters then had another slave—the baby—either to keep or sell. I know, it's unfathomably fucked-up, but it's true.

Mr. Douglass went on to explain how these mixed children of the slave owners were often treated more harshly than other slaves. This confused me. I imagined the masters would go easier on their own kids, but it was the opposite; they brutalized their own slave children worse. Why? Because of the master's wife. The master's wife was pissed! Think about it. Yes, the master is a cruel and evil bastard, but in the wife's mind, at least he's *her* cruel and evil bastard. That is, until it's revealed the master has been sneaking off and having sex with another woman, a slave no less. How do you imagine that made the lady of the house feel? Hateful, that's how.

Sometime later, the slave woman has the master's baby. The

master's wife now has, directly in front of her, a living, breathing reminder of her husband's infidelity. She was humiliated and resentful. Since she was already morally compromised enough to be involved in the ownership of slaves, it was no far leap to be extra cruel to one. That's the ugly truth about why those mixed slave children had it the worst.

Had I understood any of that before the weekend at my father's, I probably would have behaved differently. I definitely wouldn't have stood in front of my dad's wife—as his child with another woman—firing off rounds of ugly truth. I may have understood that a woman (or any off-balanced person) getting regularly physically and psychologically abused, might just enjoy some company.

My mom had gotten away. Leaving his current wife to take the brunt of his abuse. And she'd taken a lot. But she wouldn't be alone for long. She let me talk, and talk, and talk. After I'd said my piece, and was all talked out, I went to bed. And I slept great. I had no idea that when he got home, she was gonna tell him every word.

The first lash he gave me tore my skin. He had doubled over an extension cord, and used it to whip me. He'd made me take my clothes off to fully expose myself. I'd seen him beat women in a similar way. The nakedness adding to the shame and degradation.

The cord made a frightening sound as it cut through the air. I instinctively tried to cover myself, which only fueled his rage. He yelled for me to move my hands. I tried to, but self-preservation is a powerful instinct. He positioned his feet in an athletic stance. A former football standout, he was strong and powerful. He drew the cord back over his head and unleashed hell. Striking me over and over. Each blow felt like hot iron across my skin. The anticipation between strikes was its own torture. It seemed to go on forever.

I don't know where his wife was. But after reading Fredrick Douglass's book, and gaining some insight into human behavior, I'm sure she was somewhere close. On the other side of the door, perhaps? Listening? Smiling? Crying? Or maybe she was just relieved that for one day, the beatings in her home weren't hers to bear alone.

Once again, my dad handed me back over to my mom, wounded. Not only was my back raw from the lashings, but my face was numb, and my ears rang from the blows his meaty hands delivered across my face. I was hurt, but at least I'd made it out alive. My mom's boyfriend was waiting in the car. I've never been so happy to see somebody who stole money from me, before or since.

My mom filed a police report. Part of that process meant cops photographing my injuries for documentation. They made me strip and took pictures of my battered body. It felt like being violated all over again. I didn't say much through it all. But inside, I was seething. I was raging. And I was certain of one thing—I was done being anybody's victim.

CHAPTER 2

• • •

GOT MYSELF A GUN: THE DANGER OF UNHEALED PAIN

The guy never saw me coming. Something in his truck had his attention. The shopping center was busy and well lit. He was parked around the side of a building. It was darker there. In an instant I decided, *He's the one—go.* My heart thumped as I approached him. The gun was heavy in my hand. The metal felt cold against my skin. My stomach hurt. My knees felt weak. I couldn't do this, but I couldn't stop either. I felt outside myself, like a distant observer to my own actions. Leaving the light, I sank into the shadows. I opened the valve I'd been struggling to keep shut and let my pain pour out, ready to give it to someone else.

In my last few steps toward him, he looked up and our eyes met. I'm sure he felt my bad intentions. He froze. There was no turning back now. I had already taken the leap. In order to survive the landing, I was going to have to become someone else. Which was fine with me. I couldn't take much more living as who I was, anyway. If life was gonna make me fight, I was gonna fight. I swallowed hard and put my finger on the trigger.

"Gimme your fuckin' wallet!" I said. Time stopped. In that moment, the old me passed away.

I was fifteen years old when this happened. Committing a first degree felony, with a gun that I'd stolen. If I'd been shot and killed that night, the world would have said I got what I deserved. I understand that.

It's crazy to think that was me. I had no idea the seriousness of what I was doing, and even scarier, I had no idea why I was doing it. I wasn't mature enough to process what was driving my actions. All I knew was that guns don't feel. Guns are feared. Guns are respected. People know that if you mishandle a gun—*bang*. As a wounded and off-balanced boy, the gun in my hand was everything I wanted to be myself.

FEEL OR DIE

This is the risk we run when we don't face our scars. When we don't treat our wounds. They don't go away. They simply hurt us in silence. They make us strangers to ourselves and drive us to do things without understanding why. They keep hurting us until, sadly, we pass that pain on to someone else.

In order to create a safe and positive environment for your family, you need to be the one in charge. You can't let your scars or unhealed wounds determine your actions. You want what's best for your children and your partner. In order to give it to them, you've got to get right within yourself. You have to become conscious (aware) of the things you've shoved into your mental and emotional closet and tried to forget about. You have to shine a light on the darkest parts of yourself, airing them out to fully and properly heal. Otherwise, the cycle of dysfunction and passing along pain will only continue.

REEVALUATE STRENGTH

From the time we're boys, we're taught to be "tough." We're taught that our masculinity (and value as a person) is measured by our ability to withstand pain without showing it. We're taught that expressing pain—either physical or emotional—is a sign of weakness. That doing so makes us a "pussy" or a "bitch." If we try to express that something has hurt our feelings, we're often chastised or laughed at.

Regretfully, I've fallen into that trap myself. From years of competitive sports, to serving in the army, to growing up in North Toledo, calling a guy a bitch and roasting him at the expense of his vulnerability and pain is kinda what we do. Hell, sometimes it's how we show love! But this is a dangerous game with serious consequences.

We've got to be careful with suppressing how we feel. Unresolved pain doesn't just go away. It festers, lurking dormant in your spirit, often for years, until it finds an opportunity to express itself. By then, that small seed of pain has grown into a fruit-producing tree with deep and tangled roots. The fruits of that tree are poisonous and have destroyed many families. As first generation fathers, this a threat to all of us.

Nobody is immune to the dangerous effects of unhealed pain and repressed feelings. Not even the most hardened of professional soldiers. Heartbreakingly, over twenty veterans per day commit suicide in the United States. *Per day*. As soldiers, part of our effectiveness comes from being unplugged from our emotions. We do what needs to be done, and we don't feel. This is critical to a unit's ability to execute missions at a high level. Similarly, people from traumatic home lives often unplug from their feelings too. Like the soldier, they do it to survive in extreme situations.

This disconnection is effective for short periods of time. Such as, while carrying out specific missions. However, we're not meant to live like that. Holding your breath is a life-preserving skill when you're underwater. But when you come up, you've got to breathe again. If you don't, the skill that just saved your life will be the same one that kills you. Being disconnected and emotionally removed is not conducive to living a healthy and happy life. And it certainly is not a foundation upon which you can build balanced and loving relationships with your partner and children.

If you've unplugged and gone distant in order to preserve yourself, that's OK. But you've got to learn to reconnect. You've got to feel. You won't make it otherwise. The pain you're avoiding by unplugging will be replaced with an even more disorienting pain, the pain of feeling nothing. The ache of total disconnection. And for many, that pain is unbearable.

To be clear, I'm not advocating that men be whiny, wimpy, weak bodies. Of course not. We're at our best for our families when we're strong, brave, and dependable. What I'm suggesting is that we reevaluate what real strength looks like. Real strength isn't being numb to pain. Real strength is finding balance among your warrior energy, your intellectual energy, and your spiritual energy. When you learn to balance yourself in these three primal energies, you unlock your fullest potential and the strongest version of yourself. Until you learn to do that, your life is likely to be all over the place. And worst of all, you won't understand why.

NOWHERE TO RUN

When the man gave me his wallet, I took my finger off the trigger. I hadn't thought this far ahead and had no idea what to do next. The way I'd come from was well lit and heavy with shoppers. Behind the building was darkness. I sprinted into the shadows, unsure what was waiting for me there.

My chest burned from sucking in the cold November air as I ran. I could hear myself panting and the sound of dead leaves crunching under my feet. The weight of instant regret almost toppled me over.

Behind the plaza, there was a baseball field. I ran toward it. I had actually played on that field when I was younger. I crouched behind the only cover I could find, a small graffiti-covered wall. I peeked back toward the plaza. People had gathered and were pointing in my direction. Before I could think, red and blue lights splashed all over the onlookers. It was the cops.

I wasn't scared of going to jail. My home life was highly dysfunctional. I had already run away once and contemplated it regularly. The dynamics there were toxic. My mom and her new boyfriend would often get shit-faced drunk—then either fight or fuck. Both too loud for me to ignore. Both made me equally nauseous. Sometimes, as they screamed and slurred at each other, I'd get sucked into their madness. I wasn't a little kid anymore. I was done being afraid of what was on the other side of the door. If the Boogey Man was gonna eat me, I was gonna get my licks in. And I did.

Academically, I was once labeled "bright" and "gifted." Now, my grades had mostly fallen below failing. That's if I even bothered to go to school at all. I had developed a truancy record and had mastered the art of skipping. I was lashing out against the world in multiple ways. But this was a night I might never be able to recover from.

The wall I hid behind was small, only three feet high and ten feet long. It sat in the middle of a grassy area. Recent rain left the ground around it soggy with mud. I could feel myself sinking into it. When I looked down, my hands were submerged in muck. I tried to wipe them on my pants, but the mess only spread. They were too dirty to simply wipe clean. Everything connects.

From the gaggle of people, one of the police cars turned on a powerful floodlight and swept the field with it. The light stopped on the wall. I was kneeling behind it. There was nowhere to run. The car started toward me, rolling slowly off the pavement and into the grassy field. They were coming.

I felt sick. I felt nervous. I felt normal. I stayed hidden behind the wall and waited for the right time to run. Their spotlight combed the park as they drove closer to my hiding spot. I heard the car stop and a door open. An officer got out. I could hear the metal jingling from his belt as he approached the wall. I swallowed the knot in my throat and bolted.

I sprang out from behind the wall like a scared animal.

"STOP!" he yelled.

I ran with panic. I ran with heartache. I ran like if I ran fast enough, I could run into a different life. How the fuck did I get here? THIS WAS NOT ME. But, it was.

We all have to face the consequences for the decisions we make, regardless of why we made them. I was about to face mine. The officer ran after me. With each step I took, mud caked up more and more on my shoes. The ground was slowly pulling me to a stop. Behind me, the officer's keys and cuffs jingled in the rhythm of his strides. They got louder as I got slower. In desperation, I threw the gun as far as I could. My eyes welled with tears, scanning for a place to hide. But there was no hiding from what I'd done. What the cop said next convinced me the chase was over.

Very clearly, he spoke the words, "I WILL shoot you."

I believed him. And even though I wanted my life to change, I didn't want it to end.

So, I stopped.

TURNING POINT

This incident feels like it took place in a different lifetime. Since then I've gone on to graduate high school, earn two college degrees, been awarded various medals of distinction for my military service, and I've worked with some of the top healthcare professionals in the country. I've figured out how to break the cycle of dysfunction and raise a healthy and happy family. I've given back to my community by delivering inspirational talks to troubled youth in hopes I could help them better understand themselves and take ownership of their lives.

For the opportunity to turn my life around, I'd like to thank the Toledo Police Department and the officers who arrested me that night. Their calmness and professionalism in that situation kept me alive and gave a young kid the chance to figure things out. Had the officer who was chasing me panicked and shot me dead—an armed minority, who had just committed a robbery—no one would have batted an eye. In fact, many people would have hailed him as a hero.

Had my life ended that night, I wouldn't have had the time I needed to heal myself. And I wouldn't have been able to help others heal themselves either. That night, my life was in someone else's hands. And he kept me alive. So thank you.

Because I was fifteen, I was charged and sentenced as a minor. I was to serve a minimum of one year and a maximum of six years in a youth prison, several hours away. This was no boy's camp. It was for seriously troubled youth. One of the guys I got processed with was there for shooting his mother in the head. It's easy to look at a kid like that and think—*monster*. And he may be. But on the flip side, who knows what type of scars and unhealed wounds drove his actions? I doubt he knew himself.

During this low point in my life, my mom really stepped up to bat for me. We'd had plenty of conflict in our relationship, but she refused to let me fall into the abyss. When I needed her most, she fought tooth and nail for me. She got me a lawyer, she wrote the judge regularly, and she had others write letters of character reference on my behalf. She did not quit on me. And her commitment to her son earned me a second chance.

She eventually convinced the judge that my inexcusable actions were a one time lapse in judgment, and not truly reflective of my character or values. The judge decided, after a few months of incarceration, that I could be sent home. With the strict understanding that if I violated my probation, or found myself in trouble in any way, I'd be sent back to jail with no leniency.

During this whole ordeal, everyone kept asking me why I'd done it. The truth is, I wasn't self-aware enough to understand why. I was too unplugged from myself to recognize that I was hurt, angry, and confused. I didn't understand emotional and psychological scars. I said I did it for the money because, well...that's what people say. Had I understood my truth, I'd have shared it with anybody who asked. But I didn't. My actions were driven by unhealed wounds that I didn't even know existed.

As a first generation father, it's your responsibility to understand what's driving you. This will keep you from making unconscious decisions that carry catastrophic consequences. This means looking within and deepening your emotional intelligence. You have too much on the line, and too many people counting on you, to be driven by unfaced and unresolved pain. Before you can be a positive role model in your own healthy and happy family, you've got to truly know yourself.

LEARNING TO TRY

When I got out of jail, there were both old and new challenges waiting. Society had always looked down its nose at me. Now it was even worse. I felt like I couldn't go anywhere or do anything without people whispering. I'd fallen behind academically too. It was my second year of high school, but I had so few credits that I was technically still a freshman. My path to graduation—let alone anything substantial after that—looked impossibly narrow.

The purest memories from my childhood all revolve around baseball. During the summers, I'd hang out at the park all day. I'd play pick-up games with whatever friends showed up. We even made up games to play with just two or three people. After a long day of playing at the park, I'd go play my actual game with my team. On Saturdays, when my team played morning games, I'd wear my dusty uniform for the rest of the day. Usually back to the park to play more ball with the local kids.

The baseball program at my high school was serious. They didn't have any kids like me on the team. Troubled kids, teetering on the brink. I tried to play my freshman year, but my grades were so low I was academically ineligible. The coaches let me hang around, but I could never dress for the games. My sophomore year, I went to jail, and had a lot going on.

The varsity baseball coach, Rob Rose, was an accomplished and respected coach and educator. He knew I loved baseball, and he knew I needed something positive in my life. He sat me down, and we came to an agreement. I was getting a fresh start with the baseball program. Clean slate. But I had to genuinely give my best effort. Nothing else would be acceptable. From my grades, to my personal conduct, to my effort and attitude on the diamond, he was going to hold me to the highest of standards. And he did. He knew I had home life drama and issues. Challenges and struggles that other kids didn't. But none of that could matter. I'd have to take responsibility for my own actions, regardless of any of that. Coach Rose put me in a mindset of—*I have every excuse to fail, but I'm gonna succeed anyway*. That's the mindset you need to have.

As a first generation father, you've gone through things that could—maybe even should—cause you to fail in life. But that can't matter. You've got to succeed anyway. And you will! Because you're committing to success. You're prioritizing growth. You're willing to do the hard work of healing, evolving, and finding your balance. You're unwilling to accept anything other than your genuine best effort. And when that's your attitude, you've already won.

Maybe you're not where you want to be in life. Maybe you've messed up. Maybe your relationship with your kids or your partner isn't currently great. Don't be discouraged, and don't give up! Keep working at it. Rededicate yourself to improving and evolving. Take quitting off the table. Remove it as an option. And don't underestimate the cumulative—long-term effects—of genuine effort.

Coach Rose helped me understand what it meant to try my absolute best. Oddly enough, the more I tried, the more things started to go my way—often miraculously. The discipline that led to success in one area of my life led to success in multiple areas. Before long I was doing the impossible. I even found a potential path to graduate on time.

To do so, I took summer school, correspondence classes through the mail, and even got special permission from school administration to forgo my lunch period my senior year and take classes all day long. I wanted to be the first person in my family (between my mother and father) to walk across the stage as a high school graduate. And I was unwilling to accept anything other than my genuine best effort at accomplishing that goal.

My senior year was an amazing experience. I did well in school, and our baseball team was ranked high in the state polls most of the season. We shared a lot of magical moments together and won a lot of games. But more importantly, Coach Rose had taught us life lessons that would help us continue to win long after our playing days were done.

On graduation day, I sat in the crowd with the rest of my class-mates. I doubt any of them were as happy or relieved to be there as I was. A few years before, it seemed very unlikely I'd be there among them. But there I was. Cheesin'. That day cemented in my mind two things. That hard work pays off. And that I would never again accept an excuse for not trying my best. After walking across the stage, one of the first people to shake my hand and congratulate me was my grandpa. Yep, the same grandpa who once refused to even look at me. He'd become one of my biggest supporters over the years. I guess he refused to accept anything less than his best efforts too. Evolution is a beautiful thing.

SUMMARY

The scars we suffer in life have a lasting effect on us. There's no way around that. Trying to deny your pain, or disconnect from your feelings, only pushes your issues below the surface. This is a temporary fix. Eventually, unhealed wounds will make themselves felt—and it could be disastrous for you and the people you love.

Nobody else is responsible for your life. The decisions you

make are yours to own. You should see that as liberating, rather than problematic. It's freeing because no matter what environment or background you come from, you can build a better life. And if you commit to genuinely trying your best, and refusing anything less of yourself, you'll learn you can do the impossible.

CHAPTER 3

• • •

THREE PRIMAL ENERGIES: UNDERSTANDING AT ITS CORE

While plodding along on my path as a first generation father, painstakingly compiling bits of wisdom, and piecing them together to make personal improvements for my family's sake, I developed a philosophy. I'll explain it here. Learn it, and you'll attain a level of insight and balance that many fathers go their entire lives without. Embody it, and you'll free yourself—and your family—from the negative cycles of pain and dysfunction that have scarred so many of us. Master it, and you'll become an unstoppable creative force—equally successful in your personal and professional life—leaving a legacy that is a blessing to your family for generations to come. Here goes.

We are all governed by three primal energies. They are our warrior energy, our intellectual energy, and our spiritual energy. These three separate energies are the catalyst behind everything we do. They're the driving force behind all of our thoughts and actions. The quality of your life is directly related to your ability to master your three primal energies. From your marriage, to your relationship with your children, to your career, there are no parts of your life beyond the influence of these energies. Everything connects. To be a successful first generation father, to liberate your family from cycles of pain and dysfunction, your job is to work your way into the center of these three swirling energies, and root yourself there.

In this chapter, I'll explain the characteristics of each primal energy. I'll break down exactly why your ability to master a healthy amount of each energy is important to your family. And I'll detail the negative effects that come from being out of balance. Let's peel back the layers and take a deeper look.

Your warrior energy is your drive to fight. To hunt, to compete, to win. It's your ability to impose your will on a situation or an opponent. It's your refusal to lose. Everyone has to fight to get ahead. As first generation fathers, we've got to fight twice as hard. We've got to fight *against* our pasts, while also fighting *for* our futures.

Understand that the word "fight," as I'm using it here, is a metaphor. I'm not advocating you to go upside anyone's head. By fight, I mean to show toughness in the face of challenges. To persevere through pain and hardships. I mean having the guts to square off against anything that threatens the health and happiness of your family, and punching that fucker square in the nose. Metaphorically.

Over the course of building and maintaining a healthy and happy home, there will be some serious challenges. If your family is gonna survive them, you'll have to fight, and you'll have to win. There is no way around it.

Some of the challenges you'll face will be external: the rigors of everyday family life, marriage dynamics, financial stresses, etc. Some challenges will be internal: pain from unhealed mental or emotional wounds, habitual negative thinking, self-sabotaging behavior, etc. Sometimes the challenge will be having to overcome a tough situation; other times the challenge will be keeping your balance as you reach new levels of success. Both have their difficulties. Regardless of the shape your opponent takes, if it compromises your ability—or integrity—as a husband and father, you've got to fight it. And you've got to win.

You'll need your warrior, intellectual, and spiritual energies to win these battles. But be careful: imbalance in any of them can be harmful. You must learn to avoid the extremes of too much (toxic) or too little (impotent) of any of these energies. The key is balance. Let's take a look at each, and see what they look like in both their healthy and unhealthy states.

THE TOXIC WARRIOR

The toxic warrior is out of balance. Too deep into warrior energy, he sees everything as conflict. He's always looking for a fight. This lack of balance eventually turns the toxic warrior against his own family, causing him to use his fighting spirit to hurt the very people he's supposed to protect.

This person is often abusive or neglectful. Both are clear acts of aggression and hostility. In homes with toxic warrior energy, there is a constant underlying tension. At any moment, things could blow up. Family members are never really comfortable and live in fear of triggering one of the toxic warrior's episodes.

The abuse the toxic warrior dishes out can come in many different ways. Sometimes it's physical, but not necessarily. It can also be verbal or emotional. Make no mistake, hateful and harsh spoken words can be just as traumatizing as physical abuse. Sometimes, words can hurt even worse. One passive-aggressive way this toxicity expresses itself is through mean-spirited and belittling insults, disguised as "jokes." This is a manipulative attempt to put a smiley face on abuse and to dress it up as having fun.

Internal peace comes from balance. The toxic warrior is out of balance and feels no internal peace. They express their internal conflict by seeking conflict with others. They are especially irritated by those who have found a deep sense of peace within themselves.

Toxic warriors aren't dumb and are often master manipulators. They're good at masking their toxicity and putting on a healthy public persona. They may also have narcissistic tendencies. If so, they'll be experts at hurting others, then painting themselves as the victim in order to gain public sympathy. This is all part of their long play. It's a strategic manipulation in order to win the never-ending war that exists in their minds and in their hearts.

You can't build a healthy and happy home with toxic warrior energy. It can't be done. If you let yourself get out of balance in this way, your toxicity will poison your home—and everyone in it—until the situation is unlivable.

THE IMPOTENT WARRIOR

Just as off-balance, but in the opposite direction, is the impotent warrior. This man's lack of courage leaves him too scared to step up and fight, even when his family needs him to. Without the backbone necessary to persist through hardships, this person never lives up to their full potential. Life pushes them around, and they hang their head and take it.

The impotent warrior fails his family by not providing them with a sense of safety or security. They don't feel protected by him: either physically, mentally, or emotionally. He hasn't earned their trust in this way, and it chips away at their respect for him.

Even when the impotent warrior speaks words of positivity

and support, his family hears them as empty. His is encouragement from a person they don't deeply respect, so it holds little value. They know that should someone, or something, challenge his uplifting message, he'd fold. He's not willing to fully lay himself on the line for his family, and they know it.

Eventually, this person's family ends up resenting him for his lack of heart. They either disrespect him and walk all over him, or they follow his wimpy lead and become impotent warriors themselves. In both cases, he's let his family down.

Professionally, impotent warrior energy expresses itself with a lack of ambition and a lack of significant accomplishments. This person doesn't have what it takes to make big moves, even when great opportunities present themselves. His nature also negatively affects his love life. His wife, or significant other, who may have once felt safe in his presence thanks to his nonthreatening demeanor, eventually finds herself unattracted to him.

THE IMPOTENT WARRIOR PARADOX

There is an interesting paradox that sometimes happens with impotent warriors. They overcompensate for their lack of inner fight, for their weakness, by abusing those they see as weaker than them. These men often hit and bully women and children. They know, deep down, that they're scared of the world. They feel weak and small in it. They feel powerless in their lives (although they usually aren't honest enough with themselves to admit it). Rather than digging deep and committing to the honorable fight of self-improvement, these impotent warriors redirect their fear and shame by picking fights they know they can't lose.

A common way the impotent warrior paradox shows itself is through online bullying and internet trolls. Although this phenomenon isn't directly related to first generation fathers, the same principles apply. Online bullies and trolls lack healthy and balanced warrior energy. In their real lives, they often feel weak and of low influence. However, hiding behind the safety, distance, and anonymity of the internet, they can adopt a totally new persona. They become internet tough guys, making rude, disrespectful, and inflammatory comments without consequence.

Their fragile egos would defend these weak moves by saying they're just joking around, or having some fun. But in reality, they're out of balance. They're impotent in their warrior energy, and they try to overcompensate for their lack of healthy fighting spirit by being dicks, bullies, and trolls.

THE HEALTHY WARRIOR

The healthy warrior is balanced in positive fighting energy. He's an ass-kickin' gentleman. He stands tall in the face of obstacles and challenges in order to do what's best for his family. Always. He also has great discernment. He doesn't overreact, and he understands that he doesn't need to entertain every fight he's invited to.

Again—by fight, I mean dedicating yourself to overcoming an obstacle or challenge. Sometimes, the investment in time and effort it would take to win a particular battle just isn't worth it. The healthy warrior understands this and chooses his battles wisely. He's able to walk away from dumb conflicts because he knows there's a difference between having good judgment and being afraid. This keeps him from getting baited into drama and nonsense.

That said, experiencing fear is part of being a healthy warrior. As a first generation father, there are lots of things that scare the hell out of me. Questions like: can I stay happily married for the rest of my life? Can I avoid blowing up my family out of some deep-seated need for dysfunction and chaos? Can I raise happy, balanced, and principled children? Can I keep my family safe and comfortable financially? These are serious concerns. And yes, sometimes the weight of them scares me. Being balanced in healthy warrior energy doesn't mean never being afraid. It means facing your fear and having the guts to fight for what's right anyway. It means not letting fear dictate your effort.

Here are some practical ways you can tap into and strengthen your warrior energy—as it pertains to your family. Start by setting small, manageable challenges for yourself. These challenges—or goals—should be centered around your family, and they should have a concrete objective. Something you can easily confirm as completed. Such as:

- Turn off all electronics (including your phone) and spend one full hour playing and talking with your spouse and child.

- Read to your child for twenty uninterrupted minutes. If your child is older, read alongside them for twenty minutes, then spend another ten minutes talking about what you read.

- Spend two minutes before you leave bed in the morning cuddling your partner. Don't talk about schedules, obligations, or plans. Just be together for 120 seconds. Connecting. Do this before you look at your phone, or turn on the TV, or get coffee, or any of that. Put your partner first, first thing in the morning. You'll be surprised how much this simple exercise can connect you with your loved one and help you reprioritize things.

There is no limit on what your goals could be. Be creative. Just identify a specific target, and knock it down. That's it. These goals may seem small, like they don't require a ton of fighting spirit to accomplish. That's OK. You're actually laying the groundwork for something much more substantial. You're building momentum. You're establishing a standard. You're prioritizing your family, and you're making a conscious decision to give them your focused attention.

Soon, you'll be riding this momentum to much tougher wins. You'll be reopening old wounds so that they may heal properly, slaying dragons, and ascending mountains. You'll be exploring uncomfortable and unfamiliar places within yourself. You'll be deconstructing negative and damaging coping mechanisms and replacing them with healthy ones. These wins won't come easy. You're gonna have to fight your ass off. But you can and you will. Because you're a warrior balanced in healthy energy, which is exactly what your family needs from you.

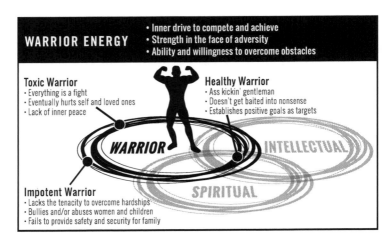

WARRIOR ENERGY
- Inner drive to compete and achieve
- Strength in the face of adversity
- Ability and willingness to overcome obstacles

Toxic Warrior
- Everything is a fight
- Eventually hurts self and loved ones
- Lack of inner peace

Healthy Warrior
- Ass kickin' gentleman
- Doesn't get baited into nonsense
- Establishes positive goals as targets

WARRIOR   INTELLECTUAL   SPIRITUAL

Impotent Warrior
- Lacks the tenacity to overcome hardships
- Bullies and/or abuses women and children
- Fails to provide safety and security for family

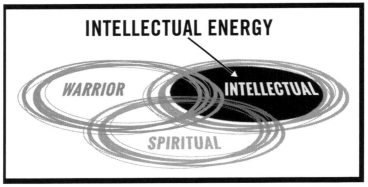

INTELLECTUAL ENERGY

WARRIOR   INTELLECTUAL   SPIRITUAL

Your second primal energy is your intellectual energy. This is your ability to think clearly and understand using logic and reason. It's your mental curiosity, your desire for truth. Your intellectual energy allows you to take information—or observations—and extrapolate meaningful connections from them.

The road to a healthy and happy home is narrow. And it's always under construction. To navigate it, you've got to be continually learning. Steadily gathering and applying new information, and increasing your proficiency at processing that information accurately. Moreover, you've got to be able to take the lessons learned from one life situation and apply those lessons appropriately in other situations. This is the essence of intellectual energy.

As first generation fathers, our intellectual energy is vital to our success. We've got to rebuild our whole idea of what a normal family life looks like. We've got to identify old, toxic patterns of seeing and being. Then, replace them with entirely new and healthy ones. Once we've done that, then comes the hard part—maintaining them. Not an easy task; you won't luck into it. It requires a lot of conscious, focused, mental effort.

Intellectual energy doesn't mean formal education. Don't confuse the two. There are lots of different ways to be smart, just like there are lots of different ways to be dumb. I think we all can agree there are some highly educated idiots walking around out there. Conversely, some of the wisest, most deeply intelligent people I've ever met have had very little formal schooling.

I'm all for education. But neither education nor professional accomplishment makes you immune to divorce, family strife, or the broken homes that stem from being off-balance. The type of smarts it takes to keep your relationship thriving and your children evolving, you don't get it from school. You get it from being awake, paying attention, and focusing your intellectual energy on self-improvement so that you might be a better man for your family today than you were yesterday.

TOXIC INTELLECTUAL ENERGY

Toxic intellectuals overthink and tend to live in their own heads. Rather than controlling their thoughts, they are controlled *by* their thoughts. This isn't good for healthy family dynamics. Real, flourishing relationships—the types you're striving to build within your family—require your mental presence. They require you to fully be with your family, not lost in neurotic overthinking.

One sign of toxic intellectual energy is that it causes you to imagine situations and challenges that don't exist. In other words, you create obstacles in your own mind. Such overthinking sabotages you and makes you less mentally efficient. It causes you to waste precious time and mental capacity creating solutions for problems that don't exist. This sort of unfocused and undisciplined thinking is a common example of your thoughts controlling you, rather than you controlling your thoughts.

Many toxic intellectuals, while overvaluing data, facts, and raw information, severely undervalue other key areas of human influence, such as emotional intelligence, a creative sense of humor, expressing interest in—or empathy for—others, etc. For this reason, the toxic intellectual is often socially awkward and has trouble genuinely connecting with people.

Being out of balance in this way is detrimental to your role as a husband and father. It hampers your ability to connect with your loved ones. It leaves you distracted, lost in thought, and worst of all, not really there—even when you're there.

IMPOTENT INTELLECTUAL

The impotent intellectual doesn't know much and doesn't care to. They don't invest any significant thought into their role in the family, and they put even less thought into how they can best serve their partner and children. They lack general curiosity and creativity. They don't ask meaningful questions, and they certainly aren't working to discover deep connections lying beneath the surface of everyday life.

Their disinterest in understanding is often worse than apathy. The apathetic person just doesn't care. The impotent intellectual is often prideful about how little they know. Their mantra is a dismissive, "I don't give a shit." They mistake this flippant, almost defiant, attitude for warrior energy. But it's not warrior energy, it's willful ignorance. And it always ends up hurting the family—in one way or another.

It requires healthy intellectual energy to see the connections between cause and effect patterns in our lives. Because the impotent intellectual isn't interested in looking that deeply, they never see how their mental laziness is harming their family relationships. This becomes a self-perpetuating cycle. The pattern goes: underachieve and disappoint the family, ignore the feedback, fail to make corrections and improvements, underachieve and disappoint more.

You can't build a healthy and happy home this way. Your family will either resent your mental flabbiness or use it to justify their own. Neither are acceptable. In order to break the chains of dysfunctional family cycles, we've got to invest ourselves in new and mind-expanding thoughts and ideas. We've got to covet growth and understanding, and balance ourselves in healthy intellectual energy.

HEALTHY INTELLECTUAL

First generation fathers balanced in healthy intellectual energy respect the power of thought. We respect deep understanding. As a result, we look for—and find—the correlation between the quality of our thoughts and the quality of our lives. Everything connects.

The healthy intellectual sees knowledge as a tool. They sharpen that tool, then use it to build better versions of themselves. They understand that intellectual energy expresses itself in lots of different ways. They look for unique brilliance in everyone—and often find it. Many times this reveals to people talents and skills they didn't even know they possessed.

Nothing is more valuable to our families than our full and undivided attention. Healthy intellectual energy allows you to focus on—and be present in—the moments of your life. This balance gives us the ability to consciously direct our thoughts. And subsequently, consciously direct our lives.

The healthy intellectual oscillates their mental focus between looking outward and looking inward. They look outward to read, listen, learn, and develop new ways of seeing. Then they look inward for ways to connect their new understandings into their own lives. Outward to apply new ideas and strategies, inward to reflect on their effectiveness. Outward to make revisions and adjustments, inward to assess how those adjustments worked. This person is always mining their experiences for new revelations and deeper understanding. Because they look for meaningful connections, they find them.

Healthy intellectual energy allows us to understand ourselves and our loved ones better. It shows us what our families need from us, and how we can best provide it. It allows us to observe the results of our decisions and actions, making corrections where needed. And it reveals deep connections that allow us to be present and focused spouses and parents.

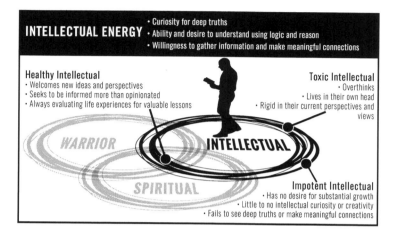

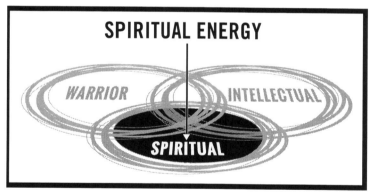

Your third primal energy is your spiritual energy. This is your connection to life itself. It's your very soul. It's your essence. Spiritual energy gives our lives a deep sense of meaning and purpose—even the hard parts. As fathers, our spiritual energy is a critical counterbalance to our warrior and intellectual energies. In order to lead your family from a place of love, strength, and grace, you need to be anchored here.

You can draw your spiritual energy from a number of different sources. Many people get theirs from religion and faith-based beliefs. If you're a religious person, and your faith brings you peace, strength, clarity, and purpose, then your religion is a great source of healthy spiritual energy for you. Rely on it often.

However, just like formal education and intellectual energy aren't synonymous, religion and spiritual energy aren't synonymous either. Religion leaves some people feeling drained, conflicted, and frustrated. This is not healthy spiritual energy. If this is you, you need to feed your spiritual energy in other ways. Music, art, hobbies, being in nature, spending time with pets, meditating, or being physically active are just a few non-religious ways some people bolster their spiritual energy.

Think of your spiritual energy like a bucket. A bucket is great for carrying water, but you've got to find a place to fill it before it does you much good. You can't be a loving husband and father with an empty spiritual bucket. It's not important (to me) how you fill it, only that you fill it. Find a well that works for you and use it. You're setting the standard for spiritual energy in your family. The people you love need to see you connected to purpose and your bucket full.

TOXIC SPIRITUAL

It may sound odd that a person can have toxic (too much) spiritual energy. But it happens. Toxicity comes from being off-balance. The spiritually toxic person has sacrificed their balance, and often their sound judgment along with it, for the sake of their spiritual beliefs and ideas. Here are a few ways spiritual energy can become toxic.

For many people, religion is the foundation for their spiritual energy. But when such a person loses their balance and slips into toxicity, their religious practices turn dogmatic, and sensible believers become zealots. Many families have been severely damaged—or totally torn apart—by fanatical religious beliefs.

Think of the parents who refuse lifesaving medicine for themselves or their children because it goes against their religion. Or the parent who disowns their child for living a life outside of the parent's strict religious views. Think of the parents who shield abusers and molesters within their institutions so their religions can save face. These things happen, unfortunately, with great regularity.

Another less ominous, but common, expression of toxic spirituality is the person who plays their life too small out of a sense of spiritual humility. There are tons of brilliant and talented people who will live and die, never having come close to maximizing their fullest potential. Why? Because they believe it's spiritually virtuous to make small accomplishments in the world and to be happy with less. To live a humble existence and to be thankful for it.

Part of me admires these folks. They tend to be genuine people who live by their values. They walk the walk of their beliefs, and I respect that. But their lack of spiritual balance does have certain negative effects. It leaves a gap that was theirs to fill.

Our human existence is all interconnected. When one of us becomes the very best version of ourselves, we all benefit. And when a person refuses to maximize their given potential, they short the rest of us. Think of the doctor who could cure cancer, but never went to med school out of spiritual humility. Or the lawyer with a natural talent and passion for freeing the wrongly convicted, but never went to law school because it seemed "too worldly." Or the artist whose work would move and inspire others, but they never chased their dream because they thought it more spiritual to stifle their talents and play life small.

Striving to accomplish all you can doesn't mean you're unappreciative of what you have. Trying to be your absolute best makes you more spiritually aligned, not less. Growing into your maximum potential is one of the most spiritually respectful things you can do. It's a way of honoring your natural gifts and talents.

As leaders in our homes, it's important that our families see us trying our best to maximize our potentials. It's also important that everyone in your home feels safe and encouraged to try their very best as well. Set the standard for continual growth and water your loved ones with encouragement and support so that they understand trying their very best is a healthy spiritual practice.

IMPOTENT SPIRITUAL

The person with impotent spiritual energy lacks the deeply satisfying peace and purpose that comes from feeling connected to something greater than themselves. With impotent spiritual energy, the world looks chaotic, disjointed, and pointless. It can seem as if there are no rewards or benefits for doing the right thing. It's impossible to lead a healthy and happy family with this worldview. Being a first generation father is hard enough. But when you don't have some core belief that gives you spiritual strength, when your bucket is totally dry, you don't stand a chance.

The disconnection spiritually impotent people feel sometimes leads to depression. From there, a whole other assortment of problems can arise, including negative habits and addictions. While these harmful distractors may temporarily ease your pain, they always make things worse in the end. No distraction or substitution can adequately fill the void that was meant to be occupied by balanced, healthy, connected, spiritual energy.

HEALTHY SPIRITUAL

Here, you're planted firmly in a sense of purpose, peace, and connectedness. You're rooted in light and spiritual wisdom. What you know, you know at a level much deeper than thought. You know it with your soul. Your intuition is healthy, and it guides you in the right directions. You know, at your core, that everything connects. You're free to live life to the best of your abilities and feel divinely called to do so.

You're a positive spiritual role model for your family. Not only have you done the work necessary to figure out exactly what fills your bucket, but you've taken the time to learn what fills the bucket of each person in your family. You create regular opportunities for them to get exactly what they need. This is true leadership—true service. And you can only provide it when you're balanced in healthy spiritual energy yourself.

I refill my spiritual bucket with laughter. With joking with the family. With staying up late and having time alone. With good food. With self-care. With exercise and meditation. With helping others. With feeling thankful. Understanding what feeds your soul is the first step to filling your bucket. And filling your own bucket is the first step to genuinely helping your family fill theirs.

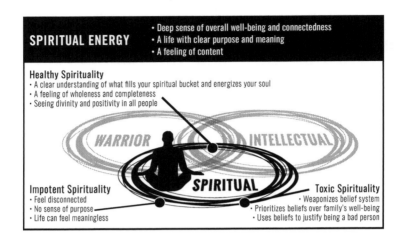

SUMMARY QUICK GLANCE CHART

HEALTHY WARRIOR	TOXIC WARRIOR	IMPOTENT WARRIOR
Fights Honorable Battles	Fights Everything/ Everyone	Won't Fight When It's Needed

HEALTHY INTELLECT	TOXIC INTELLECT	IMPOTENT INTELLECT
Uses Thoughts as Tools to Improve	Overthinks	Mentally Lazy, Disinterested

HEALTHY SPIRITUAL	TOXIC SPIRITUAL	IMPOTENT SPIRITUAL
Feels Connected, Has Purpose	Puts Beliefs Ahead of Family's Best Interests	Disconnected, Life Lacks Meaning

● ● ●

CHAPTER 4

INTERSECTIONS AND THE GOLDEN ZONE: HOW BALANCE SETS YOU FREE

Now that you understand the three primal energies, their characteristics, and the role each plays in your ability to lead your family, let's look at what happens when those energies start to overlap and intersect. As you know, life doesn't take place in a vacuum. Issues from one area typically bleed over into others. The same is true with our three primal energies.

In this chapter, I'll outline the three major intersections of primal energies. I'll describe exactly what happens in each of these zones, and explain why being balanced in just two of the three energies isn't good enough. Lastly, I'll explain what happens when you reach the pinnacle of balance that I call *the golden zone.* Hint: parenting from here is the key to raising healthy and happy children. Also, loving your spouse from here is the key to building a healthy and happy marriage. Let's get into it.

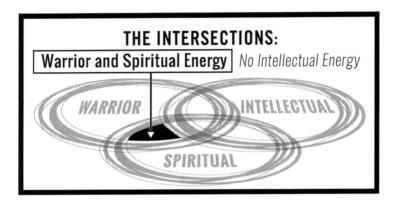

WARRIOR AND SPIRITUAL ENERGY, BUT NO INTELLECTUAL ENERGY

The person trapped in this intersection of energies is willing to—often looking to—fight for their spiritual ideas. They tend to weaponize their spiritual beliefs and use them to attack anyone who believes differently. Their lack of intellectual energy keeps them from seeing the beauty in diversity. It keeps them from understanding how different worldviews and spiritual ideologies serve all of humanity. It keeps them from understanding that different people fill their buckets in different ways. Their lack of intellectual esteem causes them to feel threatened by anything they don't understand. As the spiritual teacher Osho once said, "The less people know, the more stubbornly they know it."

Within families, well-meaning fathers can get trapped in this section. They believe they understand "the truth" and feel it's their duty to make sure their family arrives at that same understanding of "truth." However, this doesn't work. As spiritual leaders, our job isn't to force-feed our beliefs or ideas onto our children or spouses. It's to help them understand what fills their buckets, and then create opportunities for them to do so. As warrior leaders, our job isn't to hold our families hostage with our beliefs. It's to protect them from harm, and to give them the confidence to go explore life—safely—knowing they'll be loved and respected at home regardless of what they discover about themselves. This is how we should be of service to our families. This is how we should lead.

When my grandfather disowned me and my mother, that was a father caught in warrior-spiritual energy. In his heart, he believed interracial relationships were wrong. He wasn't interested in hearing any opposing opinions. He had no intellectual energy for it. When his daughter disagreed with him, he weaponized his beliefs, and cut her—and me—out of his life.

In the end, he changed himself. He got healthy, he got balanced, and he used his warrior energy to focus on growth. He expanded his perspective and learned a new, more evolved way of thinking. There were limits. I mean, he didn't expand his cable television package to include BET, but at least I was allowed inside the house. He stretched his perspective and became the father his daughter needed when she needed him most. And for that, I'm proud of him.

You're allowed to have your beliefs. You're allowed to stand up for those beliefs. I encourage you to do so. What's the point of having ideological principles if you're not willing to stand up for them? My point is simply this: to be the best husband and father you can be, you can't lock into the warrior and spiritual intersection, and totally forgo your healthy and balanced intellectual energy. It takes all three.

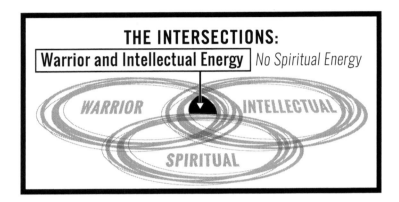

WARRIOR AND INTELLECTUAL ENERGY, BUT NO SPIRITUAL ENERGY

This person weaponizes their ideas. They're typically well-read and knowledgeable on a wide variety of topics. They're also well-spoken. This allows them to articulate arguments and spin webs with words and semantics that tangle up their opponent. Because of their lack of spiritual energy, these people often feel detached from others. They see the world as a place for competition, not cooperation. They're often cold and morally indifferent since the human moral compass is driven by spiritual energy more than intellectual energy.

Within a family, the father with warrior and intellectual—but no spiritual—energy inadvertently leads his family astray.

He teaches them to neglect their spiritual energy. He tells them and shows them that he doesn't think spiritual energy is important—or even real. He doesn't help them to discover healthy and positive ways to fill their buckets. So they don't. Eventually, they forget the bucket even exists.

This may work for a time, but ultimately, it fails. Lack of spiritual energy calls for a person to rely too much on their own understanding. It requires them to be their own higher power. No matter your belief system, we all have times in life where we need to simply trust in the power of things we cannot see. We'll need faith, we'll need grace, and we'll need the sense of purpose and connectedness that only comes from healthy spiritual energy. Without it, our warrior and intellectual energies pull us off-balance.

Some people trapped in this intersection do accomplish great things. Their warrior and intellectual energies feed off each other. This can allow them to reach lofty, prestigious positions. But without a healthy spiritual energy to keep them balanced, even this has its dangers. I've seen such people—accomplished people who don't believe in anything greater than themselves—develop a God complex.

Ironically, this person—who gets their sense of worth through their intellectual capacity—isn't as smart as they believe themselves to be. Despite all their intellectual understanding, they lack true wisdom. This is because the most meaningful understandings in life don't come from intellectual energy, they come from spiritual energy. True wisdom comes from the soul, not the mind. It comes from a deep sense of connection to universal consciousness, and from seeing others as an expression of yourself. Not from feeling separate from—and superior to—others.

INTELLECTUAL AND SPIRITUAL ENERGY, BUT NO WARRIOR ENERGY

This person is incredibly frustrating. They're smart, insightful, and have great ideas that could be valuable in both their personal and professional lives. They could be real game changers! But they're not. They habitually disappoint and underperform. This person goes through situation after situation, leaving meat on the bone, failing to maximize their potential. Meanwhile, lesser talented and lesser skilled folks are passing them by, leaving them to ask themselves, *What the hell happened? Where did I go wrong?*

What happened was a lack of healthy warrior energy! A spiritual foundation is great, intellectual understanding is awesome, but those are only two of the necessary ingredients to accomplish anything significant. You've also got to be a warrior! You've got to fight, and compete, and refuse anything other than your best effort. It takes healthy warrior energy to do hard and amazing things. And there's nothing more hard and amazing than breaking cycles of dysfunction and creating a new—healthy and happy—family legacy.

If you don't have the courage to try your best, you're doing a disservice to your family and to yourself. In the caveman days, this person would have known exactly where to hunt the best buffalo. But he'd have lacked the healthy warrior energy necessary to grab his club and go get it! Now his family's eatin' leaves for dinner and has no fur for warmth. Is that whatcha want!? Your family butt-naked eatin' leaves!? OK, that was silly. But the truth is, you aren't gonna reach your highest potential at anything in life, especially at leading a family, unless you balance yourself in healthy warrior energy.

The legendary Jay-Z once rapped the line, "I'm not afraid of dyin'. I'm afraid of not tryin'."

This is a perfect example of healthy warrior energy. As husbands and fathers, we have to be OK trying our very best and risking failure. The only thing we should fear is not giving our families our very best, and balanced, effort.

THE GOLDEN ZONE

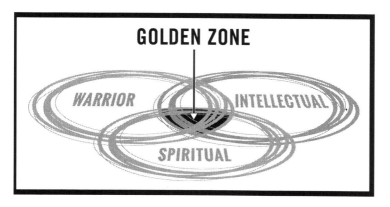

So, what happens when you put it all together? When you hit your stride, and find yourself harmoniously balanced in healthy versions of your warrior, intellectual, and spiritual energies? This sweet spot, which should be the goal for all of us, is called the golden zone. From here, there's nothing you can't do.

The golden zone is the epitome of balance and flexibility. When you're in it, you're the very best of yourself. You're grounded in excellence. You try less but accomplish more. You have access to all the healthy warrior, intellectual, or spiritual energy you may need in any given moment.

You're a deadly warrior, skilled at identifying worthy targets (setting goals) and hunting them down (accomplishing them). You're relentless in your pursuit of what's best for you and your family, but avoid unnecessary drama. You handle family conflicts with a peaceful spirit and the desire to arrive at win-win solutions.

You're also smart. You're interested in new ideas and in other people. You process information quickly and accurately. You take the disadvantages you've experienced and find creative ways to turn them into advantages that benefit your whole family. You're present where you are, and your family feels valued and appreciated.

Lastly, you feel a deep sense of spiritual connection to your life and the people in it. You feel peace, and you feel purpose. Even in the face of extreme hardships and challenges, you have faith that a greater power is working things out on your behalf. Your deep sense of well-being extends beyond intellectual understanding. You're wise, and you're well. Everything connects, and you feel it in your soul.

In the golden zone, you have full access to your highest self. Which is good. Because you're gonna need it to overcome the challenges that lie ahead.

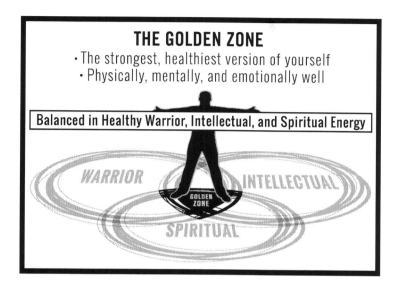

THE GOLDEN ZONE
- The strongest, healthiest version of yourself
- Physically, mentally, and emotionally well

Balanced in Healthy Warrior, Intellectual, and Spiritual Energy

WARRIOR INTELLECTUAL

GOLDEN ZONE

SPIRITUAL

IF JUST *ANYBODY* COULD DO IT...

The senior enlisted soldier in a battery (or company) sized army unit is the first sergeant. While serving in the army's 2nd Infantry Division, my unit's first sergeant had a saying. When things got tough, which they often did, he'd say, "If just anybody could do it, everybody would do it!"

This was the first sergeant's way of encouraging us. It was his way of saying that we were special. That he respected us. And that we were making a level of commitment that most people wouldn't be willing to make—or keep.

As you try to break negative family cycles and replace them with lasting positive ones, I'd like to offer those same words of encouragement to you.

If just anybody could do it, everybody would do it.

Everything about what you're trying to do is hard. Figuring out how to cultivate and maintain a healthy relationship is hard. Learning how to be a positive and continually evolving role model for your children is hard. Carving out a successful path that rewards you both financially and spiritually is hard. These tasks are hard for anyone, let alone for a first generation father. But this is the hand we've been given. We can either fold or play it to the best of our abilities. I say we play and win! And when you find yourself frustrated by the challenges and growing pains you'll face on your way to the golden zone, remember:

If just anybody could do it, everybody would do it.

CHAPTER 5

• • •

THE HEALING PROCESS: TOOLS AND TECHNIQUES FOR CONVERTING PAIN INTO GROWTH

I'll never forget the first time I saw a kid's broken bone sticking through his skin. I had just started as an X-ray tech at a children's hospital. It was my first job after graduating from radiography school. Not only was it in pediatrics (kids—which is tough), but it was also a Level 1 Trauma Facility. This meant we got the worst types of injuries and emergencies.

This particular evening, a little boy fell from a playscape and broke his arm. Bad. He screamed—partly from pain, partly from fear—as the ambulance crew wheeled him into the emergency department. His parents were visibly upset. I didn't blame them. It's jarring to see a once straight arm, now shaped like an "S." Especially when that arm is attached to your child.

When it was time for X-rays, I took a deep breath, steadied

myself, and entered the room. There was a nervous tension in the air. I introduced myself and explained exactly what I was going to do. My heart thumped in my chest, but—to my surprise—the words I spoke came out calm and confident. The anxiety running through me felt oddly familiar. It felt like home. I realized I'd been navigating through those energies all my life. Everything, from my upbringing to my time in the army, had prepared me to be strong in this moment.

His X-rays went great. Despite his serious injury, I was able to get all the images I needed without hurting him. As a reward for his bravery, I asked him if he'd prefer a Batman or a Spider-man sticker. Then I gave him both. When his parents thanked me, I could see the sincerity in their eyes. I could hear it in their voices. They felt confident that their son was going to heal and fully recover, thanks to the amazing care he received from the emergency room team.

I worked at that hospital for the next four years. In that time, I saw some of the most unimaginable traumas. I worked on kids who'd been hit by cars, mauled by dogs, shot, thrown from horses, fallen out of windows, struck by lightning, drowned, caught up in the engine of motorboats, victims of violent physical and sexual abuse, and more. It was a highly stressful environment. I dealt with a lot of parents and children during the worst moments of their lives. It was a humbling reminder of just how fragile life is.

When I first started working there, I'd come home with a new proclamation for my own kids every week.

First week: "Listen up, kids. No more trampolines."

The next week: "No more monkey bars."

The following week: "No more bikes! Y'all don't need bikes anyway. Just pretend I'm on drugs and stole all your bike money. I survived it, you will too."

Seriously though, if your children are near you now, take a break from reading this and go give them a hug. For real. I'll wait.

MALUNION

Broken arms are common in pediatric emergency rooms. A kiddo falls, extends their arm to brace themselves...and *snap*. What color cast ya want, little buddy? However, with the proper treatment and care, these breaks usually heal up good as new. With no lingering effects or issues.

One critical part of fixing a broken arm is the reduction of the fracture. That simply means lining up the broken bones so they're straight again. It's pretty gnarly, and we usually ask parents to step out of the room during that part. I've seen more than one parent hit the floor looking at their child's arm bending in unnatural directions.

Once the fracture is reduced, the bones are still broken, but now they're lined up in their normal anatomical position. From there, we cast it to keep it immobilized while it heals. And that's pretty much it. The pain meds wear off, the kiddo comes back down to earth, and the whole family is out the door with a crazy story to tell and a cast for the kid's classmates to sign.

I know, cool story. But what does a kid's broken arm have to do with being a first generation father? The connection is:

healing from trauma. We've all suffered some sort of trauma. Similar to the child with the broken arm, if we treat our injuries—and care for them properly—we can heal up good as new. But before the broken parts of us can heal, we've got to realign them.

When a broken bone doesn't heal right, it's called a malunion. A malunion (literally: bad union) can cause painful deformations, reduced range of motion, and other symptoms. When you're raised in dysfunction, you suffer emotional and mental injuries. Most of us never had those injuries treated. We weren't afforded the opportunity to heal properly. Many of us had our pain denied. We were told we weren't hurt, and threatened to be hurt more if we complained. So, we limped on, trying our best to tough it out. We developed coping mechanisms that pulled us more and more out of balance. As a result, we developed mental, emotional, and spiritual malunions.

REBREAKING TO HEAL

When a broken bone has healed incorrectly, sometimes a doctor has to rebreak it. This may sound like torture. However, in rebreaking the bone, the doctor can set it correctly and allow the injury to properly heal.

In order to be balanced in healthy warrior, intellectual, and spiritual energy, you may have to rebreak some bones. You may need to revisit some of your own improperly healed injuries. This means taking an honest and reflective inventory of your past traumas and making sure there are no malunions lurking under the surface, limiting your ability to lead and serve your family.

This exploration might hurt. That's OK. Feeling the pain is part of healing the pain. Some of you have suffered deep injuries that have been left untreated for most of your life. They're likely infected and sore. You've also likely gotten used to the pain. But being used to pain isn't the same as being healed. In the steps that follow, we're gonna work toward actual healing.

Armed with the understanding of your three primal energies, you're capable of healing and finding your golden zone of balance. You're brave, you're smart, and you're spiritually awake enough to make a full recovery from any injury, no matter how old it is. While what hurt us may not have been our fault, healing is our responsibility. This isn't something we should do. It's something we must do. We can't give the best of ourselves to our families until our splintered parts are reconnected and we're whole again.

Here's how.

THE STEPS

Early in my marriage, I would sometimes find myself feeling angry for no good reason. And when there was justification for mild annoyance, I'd be on fire. Not all the time, not even most of the time, but sometimes. And I didn't understand why.

When the kids came along, although I'd gotten better, I'd sometimes find myself parenting from a place of anger. I knew this wasn't healthy for me or my family. I committed myself to getting ahold of it and figuring out what was driving it. This meant doing the hard—and often scary—work of looking inward. Eventually, I came to understand my three primal energies and the role each plays.

The more I reflected, the more I became aware that I was off-balance. Scars and emotional malformations had pushed me into toxic warrior energy. Hence, I was ready to fight. About anything. That imbalance had served me well in overcoming my early life challenges. I needed an abundance of warrior energy to survive. My toxic warrior energy also served me well in the army. But now, while trying to maintain a healthy and loving relationship with my wife, and raise happy and well-adjusted children, that imbalance no longer served me. I had to evolve.

This meant committing myself to balance and healing. It meant stretching my intellectual energy by reading positive books and listening to smart, positive people talk. It meant preserving my mental peace by fencing off the garden of my thoughts and not just letting any ole trashy idea wander through it. It meant paying close attention to what actually filled my spiritual bucket, and doing more of that. Unapologetically. It meant anchoring myself in peace, rather than anchoring myself in a fight. It didn't mean totally abandoning my warrior energy. It just meant finding balance and becoming whole. The following steps helped me:

- **Acknowledge Your Feeling**. I noticed and acknowledged when I felt angry. This is important. For any of this to work, you must be honest with yourself. If you're feeling a certain way, but deny it, you close off the road to resolving the deeper, underlying issue. And you have no chance at healing it.

- **Give it Space**. After I've recognized I'm angry, it's important I spend some quiet time alone. In that time, I just let the feelings be. I don't try to talk myself out of them. Some people might call this reflective time "meditation," some might call it a nap—I do fall asleep during it sometimes—but the title isn't important. What's important is giving the feelings the space to exist without judging them.

By observing your strong negative emotions, you're lessening any subconscious grip they may have on you. By letting them exist now, you're preventing them from being suppressed, and then springing up on you later. Also, sitting quietly and reflecting on your feelings keeps you from saying or doing anything in the heat of the moment that you'll regret later. You're doing the wise work of dealing with your internal feelings first, and not the external cause of them.

· **Find the Real Trigger.** Only after I've done steps one and two, do I move on to step three: identify the trigger. This takes insight, self-awareness, and honesty. A lot of people don't see what's *really* triggering their emotional reactions because they don't see themselves clearly. They're out of balance, so their ability to make deep and meaningful revelations is limited. They see the symptoms but not the cause. This part may be painful. Here's a personal example.

I had to revisit some painful experiences from my past before coming to the revelation that I had issues with perceived disrespect. Due to some of my early life experiences—such as having a low social standing since birth—I was highly, sometimes irrationally, sensitive to perceived disrespect.

This insight was so revealing. It helped me understand myself, and instantly made it easier for me to move toward balance. I leaned more on my intellect and spiritual energies, and worked toward consciously understanding what was happening to me when I felt triggered. I was taking my power back.

Over time, I was able to heal this issue. It didn't happen overnight, and it took work. As the saying goes, it's a process—not an event. But when you're able to really get to the source of an unhealed injury, when you're able to face it while maintaining your balance in all three of your primal energies, it's just a matter of time before you heal it.

- **Remember the Real You.** At this point, you've identified a malformation, and the fracture that caused it. In the personal example I'm using, my malformation was an oversensitivity to perceived disrespect. It was caused from a string of early life events where I was seen as lower or lesser than others. Once you're able to see yourself this clearly, you're almost free. The next step is simply remembering that you are not the feelings you're experiencing, *you're much more.*

One of my favorite spiritual philosophers, Eckhart Tolle, teaches that our true identity isn't found in our thoughts or emotions. Rather, our true identity is found in the consciousness—the awareness—that *observes* our thoughts and emotions. Kinda wordy, but dope. If you're looking for some interesting and different spiritual reading to check out, I like his stuff. He's helped me fill my bucket more than once.

I agree with Eckhart here. Once we detach our identity from our thoughts and emotions, they lose their power to pull us all over the place. We can then be proactive about our thoughts, rather than reactive. Here, we're no longer at the mercy of our ever-changing emotions. We're no longer driven by subconscious needs to protect untreated, inflamed, and infected wounds. Your malunion will have fully and properly healed.

- **Share Your Discovery.** Sharing your healing with others is the icing on your evolutionary cake. Talk to your family and friends about what you're doing. Talking it through will benefit you both. Putting your discoveries into words will help you clarify the connections you've made. It will also help you understand the revelations you've discovered much deeper than when they exist only in your mind. What you've just done is amazing. Tell somebody about it!

Also, by sharing your story of healing and growing, you'll be encouraging friends and family to evolve too. You'll be leading from the front and potentially helping them face their own scars and heal their own traumas. Your ability to heal can have a positive impact and influence on everyone around you.

Your personal healing strengthens your entire family. Not just your current family either, but your family for generations to come. When your children see you working to improve and find your balance, you're teaching them to do the same. Passing these lessons down through generations, rather than scars, is the ultimate example of positive family leadership.

ALCHEMY

I love reading books on self-improvement and the power of the mind. One influential book I read was *The Alchemist*, by Paulo Coelho. Alchemy, I've since learned, is the ancient study of transforming one substance into another. The idea is that by removing an object's impurities, it can be transformed into something else, something better. Although the practice of alchemy had various branches, it was most famously used in attempts to transform lead into gold. Sounds impossible, right? Transforming a hunk of ugly lead into precious gold? Well, you're wrong. It is possible. I know because I've done it. And I'm about to show you how to do it too.

The first step in turning lead into gold is identifying what your "lead" is. What's a heavy, ugly, hunk of metal in your life that you'd like to transform into something valuable? My lead was the dysfunction I grew up with and the scars it left. Your lead might be anything. So, ask yourself, what's something heavy—maybe even painful—in your life that you'd love to be free of? Only you can know what it is for sure. But you can't flip it into something valuable until you identify it.

Once you've clearly identified a single piece of lead that you'd like to transform into gold, say it out loud. For me, it was *I want to stop the cycle of family dysfunction*. Just like in discussing your healing discoveries, speaking your lead out loud brings clarity to your thoughts. It puts the lead in focus and allows all your energy to take aim at it. Once you've done that—abracadabra—it's time to flip that sucker into riches. How? I'm glad you asked.

THE APPRECIATION TRANSFORMATION

In the alchemy I use, appreciation is the magic elixir. Appreciation changes everything. It unlocks the gold hidden inside of our lead. It turns our scars into sources of power. It turns the injuries we've suffered (even the self-inflicted ones) into strength and balance. The secret to turning lead into gold is learning to appreciate the lead.

I've been practicing this technique for years. When I'm at my best, every time something goes wrong in my life—be it big or small—I'm confident I can transform it into something valuable. Into gold. I do this by getting myself to a place where I'm genuinely thankful to have the lead. I'm appreciative of whatever hardship or challenge is in front of me. I'm appreciative because I know the challenge has—buried inside of it—a lesson. And I'm thankful for the lesson, even before I know what it is. Being thankful for the lesson requires being thankful for the problem. And if you're thankful for the problem, you don't *have* a problem! Suddenly, all you're left with is the lesson. Just like that, lead has become gold.

I understand that when something hurts us, the last thing we wanna do is "feel appreciative" of it. That advice can sound like some New Age bullshit. We're real people with real problems—and real human emotions. On top of that, the problems we face have very real consequences for us and for our families. I get it. But I wouldn't waste your time if this didn't work. I wouldn't waste mine either. It does work. And I use it regularly to turn shit into shine. All this alchemy process requires is that you proactively decide you're going to feel appreciative about something hard, or hurtful, or challenging. Which is easy to do if you're balanced in your golden zone.

Let your warrior energy fight *against* feeling sorry for yourself, and fight *for* transformation. Let your intellectual energy observe the lead from every angle, looking to make deep and valuable connections on how to learn and grow from it. Let your spiritual energy give you faith that this obstacle is really a gift, here to make you better, stronger, smarter, and more balanced.

This book is an example of how alchemy has worked in my life. By becoming appreciative of my family dysfunction, and balancing in my three primal energies, I found ways to break the cycle. By continuing to be appreciative for each discovery I made—no matter how long it took to uncover—I was able to make even deeper revelations and connections. I was inching toward my golden zone and gaining momentum.

Over time, I purified my attitude from judgment and resentment to genuine appreciation for all the dysfunction I had been exposed to. It turned out to be a gift, one I would use to help other people break their own cycles of dysfunction and negative family patterns. My golden zone insight showed me that through all the chaos, I had been getting exactly what I needed, exactly when I needed it.

Once I mastered the art of alchemy, the scars that once hurt me—and the steps I took to overcome them—became the basis for this whole book. Appreciation has transformed my lead into valuable lessons that strengthen me and my family. And it has also put me in the humble position to help others get their bags in order too. If that ain't turnin' lead into gold, I don't know what is.

PRACTICE, PRACTICE, PRACTICE

Mastering this technique takes practice. When we think a thought, it actually leaves a little pathway in our brains. This is another trick our bodies do to run more efficiently. These pathways allow our brains to react to familiar situations quicker, and without occupying much mental power. The more we think a thought, the more established those particular pathways become. This is how we're able to do the things we do often, like driving home, without even thinking about it.

The problem with this shortcut is, if you've established negative reactions to certain situations, you'll tend to react negatively every time a similar situation arises. This is why change is so hard. Changing your mind can literally mean having to change your mind.

Establishing new and positive reactions to those situations requires focused, concentrated effort. Imagine your new little thought, wielding a machete, hacking through the jungle of your mind, trying to establish a new path. The more it walks that path—the more you practice this new thought—the more established the pathway becomes, and the easier it is to access. Work at it long enough, and you'll establish a new default way of thinking.

Now, when a hunk of lead falls into your life and conks you on the head, you know that you have the power to transform it. When you're balanced in your healthy primal energies, and you look at your lead through the lens of appreciation, there is no challenge in your life that you can't turn into gold.

A final word on the topic. The appreciation transformation isn't meant to be some form of denial. It doesn't mean suppressing your true feelings. That's being disingenuous, and you can't be in the golden zone like that. You'll only frustrate yourself if you pretend to be appreciative of something that's upsetting you. Don't try to fake it till you make it. Rather, start with small inconveniences and look for new ways to see them. When you get a little momentum behind you, look for slightly bigger challenges to be thankful about. Keep this up, and before long, you'll learn to see the most traumatic events of your past as your biggest blessings.

GET INTO THE GOLDEN ZONE

Now that you understand your three primal energies (warrior, intellectual, and spiritual), let's look at them in the context of this chapter and see how each energy will help you heal.

Warrior Energy: It takes bravery, strength, and courage to face your pain. Therefore, only the strongest of warriors ever truly heal.

Intellectual Energy: To heal your wounds, you've got to understand them. Focus your intellectual energy on looking inward and seeing yourself clearly. Consume positive messages and limit mental junk food. Understand that creating new ways of seeing and thinking takes conscious effort in the beginning. You're proactively reprogramming your thought patterns in a way that best serves you and your family.

Spiritual Energy: Healthy spiritual energy has the power to transform lead into gold. Release negativity and practice appreciation. This will give you the magical ability to turn your worst scars into your biggest blessings.

The Golden Zone:

- Face Your Pain

- Consciously Create Your Thoughts

- Appreciate Lead into Gold

CHAPTER 6

● ● ●

FIRST GENERATION HUSBAND (PART 1)

WHAT IS LOVE?

For decades people have debated: is love an emotion, or is love an action? Is it something you feel? Or is it something you do? In this chapter, I'll explain what I've learned about what love is and what it isn't. I'll even share with you my personal formula for love. It's the litmus test I use to determine if I'm acting out of love, or if I'm acting out of some lesser motivation.

You may be wondering why a book on fatherhood has dedicated an entire chapter to understanding love. There are two reasons. The first is because the cornerstone of a healthy and happy home is a loving relationship between the parents. In fact, as first generation fathers, learning how to truly love your partner is the most important thing you can do for your child. That's right. Loving your child's mother well, loving her thoroughly, loving her *fully*, is the best gift any father can give his child. Give your children this, and everything else will take care of itself.

The second reason for this chapter is the principles of genuine love—the love we'll talk about here—apply to loving your children as well as your spouse. For many of us, our understanding of love has been warped and deformed. In this chapter, I'll help you regain a clear understanding of what healthy love is. You shouldn't be giving your spouse, or your children, anything less.

So what is true love? Here's the formula I use.

Love = Action + The Intention Behind the Action

What does this mean? It means love is what you do. It's the way you treat a person. The way you support and encourage them. The way you value and appreciate them. The way you cherish and respect them. In this sense, love is very much an action.

But true love is more than just what you do, it's also why you do it. It's the intentions behind your actions. To determine if you're acting in true love, ask yourself: are my intentions here to serve my partner's best interest? Or, in actuality, are you using what looks like loving actions to serve your own interest? All acts that look loving are not created equal. In order to express genuine love, both your actions and intentions must be loving.

As a newlywed, I read a book called *The Road Less Travelled* by Dr. M. Scott Peck. He argued that real love is something we consciously do in order to facilitate growth in someone else. I'd never thought of it like that. As a product of my environment, my understanding of love was pretty rough around the edges. This new idea caused me to look inward, and face the hard truth that I hadn't focused much intellectual energy on understanding genuine love.

I was married. But I knew nothing about the type of healthy love that facilitates growth in someone else. The type of love that could enrich two people for an entire lifetime. So, I worked to find more balance in that regard and inched closer to my golden zone.

Today, Sarah and I have been together for over twenty years. Our relationship is stronger than ever. In order to get here, we've had to learn a lot about ourselves and each other. But most importantly, we've had to work hard to help each other grow and evolve into our own golden zones. Dr. Peck would say that part—the facilitating growth in one another—is true love.

LOVE IS ACTION

There's a reason the phrase—actions speak louder than words— is so popular. Because it's true. Showing love to our significant others—or children—starts with what we do. Loving words are nice. But words without action mean nothing.

Our acts of love don't need to be grand; they just need to be genuine. For example, when Sarah comes home, I try to greet her at the door. This simple act costs nothing, but it makes her feel welcomed and valued at home. It immediately communicates, *you are loved here*. Which is exactly how home should feel.

Remember, your children are watching everything you do. When I greet Sarah, the kids are usually right there under our feet, smiling at her, and eagerly sharing their highlights from the day. Don't underestimate how powerful these moments are. Finding small ways to express genuine love to your spouse—and letting your children see it—is magic. It shapes your child's idea of what home is, of what family is, of what love is. Take your responsibility in creating those experiences seriously.

Any act of love must be positive. If it ain't positive, it ain't love. Many abusive and manipulative relationships tangle love and pain together, confusing the two. Some people from toxic environments even think love should hurt. This is dangerous and wrong. If it hurts, it ain't love.

This is true of both actions and words. Love never speaks harmful, hateful, demeaning, disparaging words. Love always builds a person up, it never tears them down. Love flows through peaceful and cooperative energy. It never flows through violence or anger. It encourages and strengthens, never belittles or degrades.

Sadly, some of our deformed malunions have warped our idea of love so bad it's barely recognizable. Some people are so scarred they aren't comfortable with positive love. They don't like or want it. They hurt their loved ones and—whether they realize it or not—they want their loved ones to hurt them back. This is a devastating way to live, and it cripples our ability to create healthy homes for our families. As husbands, and as fathers, we must do everything in our power to protect our family from this harmful and backward perversion of love.

LOVE IS INTENTION

The action part of the love formula is pretty straightforward, but what's driving your actions? Why are you doing what you're doing? Intentions are easy to mask. They're also easy to misunderstand. Let's look at a situation from my personal life, and see how intention determines if an act is love or not.

Scenario: My beautiful and talented wife puts a load of her laundry in the washing machine. But, as she often does, she gets busy doing other stuff, then falls asleep for the night. Me, the night owl, remembers her clothes in the washing machine. While she sleeps, I dry them, fold them, and hang what needs hanging. I pile them neatly on the stairs for her to put away the next day. The question is, was that an act of genuine love? Let's apply the formula.

Action: Was that act itself positive and helpful? Hell yeah, it was! Who wouldn't appreciate their laundry being folded for them? So, it was definitely an act of genuine love, right? Well, not so fast.

Intention: What were my intentions behind the act? Does it make a difference? Absolutely. For example, if I did it to help her, to make her life a tad bit easier, to show her I've got her back even down to the smallest of tasks, then yes. It was an act of genuine love.

But, what if my intentions weren't so pure? What if I folded her laundry in order to get something in return? Or, as happens often in relationships, what if I did it to be passive-aggressive? As a way to call attention to a perceived imperfection? The intention makes all the difference.

With one intention, I'm telling her, "Babe, I got you. It's me and you against the world!"

With the other, I'm saying, "You forgot your shit, AGAIN! Don't worry, I'll fix it."

Same act, different intentions. One is love; one is war.

In order to give your partner—or your children—the quality of love they deserve, you've got to commit loving acts freely and consistently, and you've got to do so while holding loving intentions in your heart. That's the formula.

LOVE LIVES IN AWARENESS

One reason love is so difficult to attain is that it only lives in awareness. True love for someone (including for yourself) can only exist in a heightened state of consciousness. Lasting, healthy, happy relationships require a continual *waking up*. This process of waking up, of growing, of balancing yourself in the golden zone, is uncomfortable. This makes sense. After all, they're called growing "pains," not growing "this feels greats."

But if you want to learn how to truly love, you have to keep waking up, despite the pain. You have to keep stretching yourself, keep mastering yourself, keep balancing yourself in your primal energies. Keep healing so your actions aren't being driven by underlying dysfunction and scars.

The good news is that as you grow personally, your capacity to love grows too. Don't let the discomfort of growth dissuade your evolution. Staying the same hurts worse in the long run. Even relationships started with low-level awareness, and rooted in self-interest, can evolve into genuine love, if you're willing to work on yourself.

ME OR THE SYSTEM

Sarah and I have taken a very nontraditional path to get where we are. We met in college, and it was immediately clear that she and I came from different realities. She had graduated

with honors from an expensive private high school in the sub-
urbs of Upstate New York. Her father was an engineer. Her
parents had been married all of her life. She was an artist. She
had no scars.

Then there was me. It took a herculean effort for me to
graduate high school. With zero plans for college—and zero
resources—I got an unexpected and miraculous offer to attend
the Savannah College of Art and Design to play baseball.
My older brother (from another mother) was in prison. My
father was in prison. I'd been in juvenile prison, and now, I
was suddenly in college. Talk about a culture shock. Sarah
had an assortment of career options in front of her. I had no
idea what I was doing with the next day of my life, other than
baseball practice.

Despite our significant differences, she and I shared a lot of
the same values. For example: hard work. Sarah was the most
committed student I'd ever seen. She took trying her best very
seriously. An attractive quality, one that she still holds today. I
was equally serious about my commitment to outgrowing the
shadow of my past. We were very different, yet somehow, an
oddly perfect match.

We dated for years, learning to trust each other and earning
each other's respect. But college is a transitional time in life.
It's not supposed to last forever. When I graduated, I was
faced with a sobering question: now what? I hadn't gone to
school with a long-term goal. I went because an opportunity
presented itself, and it seemed like the right thing to do. It
was an escape from any negativity and drama at home. But
I was out of my element, and had no clue how to prepare for
real life after school.

I'm older than Sarah. So when I graduated, she still had classes to take. Unsure what to do next, I hung around the scene for a while. As my peers eagerly packed up and moved on to their adult lives, I drug my feet, partied, and tried to hang onto the moment. Before long, though, I began to feel rudderless. I wasn't moving toward anything. I was off-balance, and needed to make a move. I needed to do something with myself.

I decided to join the army. I had too much warrior energy to burn off still, and I'd hoped committing to something bigger than myself would help me find my balance. The army would certainly provide my life with some structure and goals to work toward.

Sarah was tearing through school and en route to graduating summa cum laude. Our relationship, which had become on again-off again, was at a crossroads. We loved each other, but our future was uncertain. Maybe we were just too different to enter the next stage of life together. Maybe our relationship had run its course.

I signed my army contract in Savannah, Georgia. I asked my recruiter to send me someplace far away. He smiled and said, "I can do that." I loved Sarah. But I'd convinced myself that I wasn't the right type of guy for her. We'd had fun, but I wasn't what she needed for the upcoming—adulthood—part of her life. In my mind, what she needed was a "system guy." When I left the recruiting station, my contract was signed. After basic training, I was going to spend a year in South Korea.

What do I mean when I say Sarah needed a "system guy"? I mean she needed a guy whose background, upbringing, and future prospects mirrored hers. A private school guy, who'd never come close to being killed by the police. A guy with a clear trajectory and a five, ten, and twenty-year plan in his mind. A guy with no scars. Not a guy who was gonna spend the next twenty years of his life trying to figure out ways to heal himself and break the cycles of family dysfunction and trauma, like me.

Fortunately, I was wrong. Sarah didn't want a system guy. She wanted me, scars and all. So, we took a gamble. We bet on each other. Without telling a soul, we went to the Chatham County Courthouse, and we got married. It was just her and I. In fact, when the Justice of the Peace said he couldn't make the marriage official without at least one witness, we asked the county clerk—who happened to be sitting at her desk—if she would do us the honors. She agreed. And we officially became husband and wife.

I'm not suggesting others do what we did. Everybody's situation is unique. But our secret little courthouse wedding worked perfectly for us. It was symbolic of our commitment to each other regardless of anyone else's approval, input, or presence. It was just us, joining our two very different worlds together. It was me showing her that although I didn't know what my future would look like, I wanted her in it. And it was her showing me that she chose me over a system guy, and over the whole damn system itself. It put us on an equal playing ground and solidified us in our battle. It was us against the world.

All these years later, we're still fighting for each other. I'm still trying to find ways to be better for her and for our kids. And she's still growing into her fullest, most badass self. She's still the hardest worker I know. We've spent the last twenty-plus years growing together, learning from each other, challenging each other, and helping each other evolve. Love is a beautiful thing.

THE SADDEST REASON LOVE FAILS

Marriages fail for lots of different reasons. However, I find it particularly sad when a marriage ends because one (or both) of the people in the relationship lose themselves. Society has romanticized the idea of love so much that real people can't live it. Life isn't like a movie. And if you walk around with the expectation that it is, you're going to be sorely disappointed. Romanticized love says we're supposed to totally lose ourselves for it. But that's a lie. Real love will always help you find more of your authentic self, not lose it. If you've lost yourself in what you're doing, what you're doing isn't love.

It's sad when people give up on their dreams and aspirations in life because they think that's what love requires. It's not. Losing yourself isn't how you set the foundation for a healthy and lasting marriage. It's how you set the foundation for regret and resentment. We all love our families. And we all play various roles within them. But if you totally sacrifice yourself to those roles, you'll end up holding it against the very people you love the most.

The common misconception that love means forgoing your own individuality has led to a lot of unhappy homes and failed relationships. What true love requires is balance. If you sacrifice your own individuality out of some misguided notion that that's what your family needs from you, you're giving away the one thing your family can't get anywhere else in the world—you. Yes, they need you to play your role within the family dynamic, and they need you to play it well. But that can't be the totality of your existence.

They also need you to be alive! They need to see you chasing dreams and exploring life. They need to see you trying new things, struggling, adjusting, and persisting. Nothing zaps a person of their vigor and passion for life like taking away their individuality. Your family doesn't need you to be some cardboard cutout dad from a Father's Day commercial. They need you to be *you*.

Ladies, this is especially true for you. Nobody sacrifices and gives themselves away quite like wives and mothers. Yes, loving your family is important. But please understand, in order to do what is absolutely best for your family, you've got to balance loving us—with loving yourself! With maintaining your own sense of identity. With keeping you—you. If you give all of yourself away in the name of "love," there will be nothing left of you in the end.

Both parents need to understand the children aren't just watching Dad, they're watching Mom too! Both sons and daughters need to see their moms striving for things, facing fears, overcoming challenges, and continually setting the standard for how a properly loved woman lives a full life. Moms, you can't show them those things if you totally forgo your own life to simply cheer them on in theirs. The trap of losing yourself now will lead to resentment later. Don't fall into it. Stay balanced. Stay you. And remember:

True love is not losing yourself.

Warrior Energy: Focus your warrior energy on dismantling old, unhealthy ideas about love.

Intellectual Energy: Keep refining and updating your idea of what healthy love looks like. Read about it, talk about it, ask people whose judgment you trust for insight. Within your relationship, audit the intentions behind your actions. Be honest about what's driving you. A genuinely loving act must be done with loving intentions.

Spiritual Energy: True love is a spiritual connection. It's a divine experience. Treat your loved ones—and your relationships with them—with the reverence they deserve.

The Golden Zone:

- Overcome Negative Norms

- Clarify Your Vision of Healthy Love

- See Love as Divine

CHAPTER 7

● ● ●

FIRST GENERATION HUSBAND (PART 2)

FROM FINDING THE RIGHT PARTNER TO MAINTAINING YOUR MARRIAGE

For some of you at this point in the book, you already have a child but aren't together with the child's mother. Your focus may be how to have a loving relationship with the mother of your children, even though you aren't romantically in love anymore. Others may be starting from scratch on how to build a new marriage and strong relationship for a family. And for those whose marriage is doing well, the goal is to ensure you are maintaining and improving it, especially as the pressures of parenting come into play.

One of the most important decisions you'll ever make in your life, maybe THE most important decision you'll ever make, is who you start a family with. If you've made the unfortunate mistake of marrying—or having a child with—the wrong person, you know just how right I am. In this chapter, I'll break down what type of characteristics (emphasis on the word "character") you should be looking for in a potential partner. Then I'll give you my most valuable insight on how to help your spouse find—and get into—their own golden zone.

First things first, let's spend a little time discussing what to look for in a mate.

FINDING WIFEY: WHAT TO LOOK FOR IN A SPOUSE

What type of qualities should you look for in a wife? And no, this isn't me asking if you're a boob man or a butt man. This is a serious question that lots of guys spend too little time thinking about. As men, we're naturally visually stimulated creatures. I get it, the female form is gorgeous. But when it comes to finding a wife, choosing a life partner—and a mother for our children—you'd be a damn fool to prioritize looks over character. Still, it happens every day. Dude falls for some hottie, and the next thing you know, he's followed his dick down the wedding aisle. But marriages based strictly on physical attraction almost never last. The everyday pressures of marriage and parenthood are too much.

So, if you shouldn't marry her just because she's the best-looking woman who'll have you—or because she can twerk in a handstand—then what are some of the qualities you should be looking for in a wife? Here are my top five.

1. **Moral Character**: A woman of high moral character has the virtuous traits of integrity, responsibility, honesty, and loyalty. These are the most important qualities a life partner can have. Think about it: marriage is a legally binding partnership with another person. And if it bears a child,

you're linked together forever. Her moral character is everything.

I've seen guys get played by women who cheat, lie, put the children in bad—flat-out dangerous—situations, and basically try to extort money out of the dad before letting him see his child. To keep it 100, there are some shady-ass chicks out there. Stay awake. Because if you cuff yourself to one, it's just a matter of time until she screws you over. This is why—to me—there's nothing more important in a life partner than moral character.

2. **Compatibility**: This means being able to coexist without problems or conflict. Compatibility is huge in a marriage. Two good people—both of high moral character—can still get on each other's damn nerves. Just because you're both great people doesn't mean you're gonna be a great couple.

    It takes honesty to assess compatibility. If either of you is faking who you are, or pretending something doesn't bother you when it actually does, you can't genuinely assess your compatibility with each other. Sometimes people pretend while they're dating. But marriage is too long to pretend. The truth eventually comes out. Do yourself a favor, be honest early in relationships. If you're not compatible, it's better to know early rather than later.

3. **Priorities**: You need a partner with similar life priorities. Someone with your same general sense about what's most important in your shared lives. For example, if you prioritize hard work and seeking to continually improve your circumstances, you need a partner with similar goals. Having priorities that don't align stresses a relationship. It

pulls people in different directions. And if the priorities are out of sync for too long, the relationship eventually breaks.

A common mistake here is marrying someone, then hoping their priorities change after marriage. They won't. If you married a partier, don't be surprised when they still prioritize partying after marriage. You don't buy a four-door car, then later get upset at it for not being a truck. If you want a truck, get a truck. Marrying someone with the hopes you can change them (or their priorities) later is an old and tired cliché. It doesn't work, and has led to a lot of failed relationships. Now, people can—and often do—change. But only if *they* want to change. Not because you badgered them into it.

4. **Chemistry:** Chemistry is simply attraction. It's that draw, that spark. It's usually why we start dating a person in the first place. There's a catch-22 about chemistry, though. It's an important thing, but it's not the only thing. You need it, but it's not enough to sustain a healthy and happy marriage on its own.

   That said, one of the quickest ways to spell doom for your marriage is to let your chemistry fizzle out. So once you've got her, don't get lazy. Don't get complacent, and don't take her for granted. Doing so will kill your chemistry dead. And without that spark, you're nothing more than roommates. So keep doing the things you did to get her, while also finding new ways to fuel your chemistry. That'll keep your relationship fresh and fun, for both of you.

5. **Ride or Die:** This phrase describes someone who stays loyal to the end, regardless of how big a problem you face.

Every relationship has problems. Even the best of them. You need someone you know is gonna ride through the tough times with you, and not bail when the road gets bumpy.

When Sarah and I exchanged vows in a small courthouse room, we committed to be ride or die for each other. Since then, we've faced challenges and uncertainties of all sorts, knowing only one thing for sure—no matter what happens—we're ride or die.

When you have two people with this mentality, and this level of commitment to each other, they become a force that can accomplish whatever they set their sights on. There is nothing that they can't overcome. Together. As first generation fathers, there's a lot for us to learn. We're gonna make mistakes as we grow and evolve. You need a partner who understands that, respects your efforts, calls you on your bullshit, and keeps it movin'—steadily forward. You need a ride or die.

These are the top five qualities I prioritize in a life partner. Do you have any of your own that are different? There is no right or wrong answer, other than not thinking about it at all. Do that, and you'll likely find yourself learning a painful lesson one day.

Now, some jaded souls will tell you it's impossible to find a partner like this. But that's not true. People like this find each other every day. But there's a trick to it. Would you like to know what it is?

The trick is, don't focus on finding a person with these high-quality characteristics. Instead, focus on being a person with these high-quality characteristics yourself. Be all the things you hope to find in someone else. You want to attract someone of high moral character? You be of high moral character. You want to attract someone who has their priorities straight? You have your priorities straight. You want chemistry with someone who doesn't bail at the first sign of trouble? You be that person yourself. That's the trick. Forget looking for what you want, focus on becoming what you want, and the rest will take care of itself. Everything connects. It's really that simple.

Once you've found the person you want to love forever, here are some valuable tips that'll keep your relationship thriving over the years. They'll help you and your partner elevate your entire relationship into the golden zone.

HEAR HER

Of all the things I do to show Sarah I love her, she says what makes her feel most loved and valued is the way I listen to her. If you want your marriage to thrive, you *have* to listen to each other. This is more than just hearing the words being said. It's understanding the spirit, the essence, of what the other person is communicating. Nothing validates a person—and makes them feel respected and important in their relationship—quite like making them feel heard.

Good listening can be boiled down to one word: attention. A good listener gives their undivided attention, and listens with the intent to understand. A bad listener does the opposite. They're distracted and not invested in what's being said. They don't really care to understand, and are often just being quiet until it's their turn to talk. This isn't effective communication and doesn't lend to a healthy environment. It's rude at best and flat-out disrespectful at worst.

Much like your ability to love, your ability to listen is also directly related to your level of awareness—of consciousness. Listening well requires quieting your mind to distractions and competing thoughts, and being present where you are. You can't listen when you're mentally distracted. You can't be two places at once. If you want to fortify your relationship, and express your respect for each other in a simple way, learn to be good listeners.

A big part of listening is asking open-ended questions.

- What's on your mind?

- How do you feel about that?

- Tell me about it.

These prompting questions set the stage for your partner to open up and communicate with you. It takes some practice to develop a good subtle technique. You don't want your conversations to come off as an interrogation. But even when you're not the best at it, the message is still being conveyed to your partner: I value your thoughts and opinions, and I want to hear them. Which translates to your partner as: I value you. I love you. I'm trying. I care.

FAN HER FLAMES

Remember, leadership is service. One important way to be a leader in your marriage is to encourage and inspire your partner into their own balanced, golden zone. Speak words and take actions that fan the flames of their passions. Help them expand intellectually by exploring their interests with them and letting them teach you things. Walk with them as they fill their spiritual bucket, however that may be.

This will benefit your partner by allowing them to feel alive in their individuality. It'll benefit your children by showing them that healthy love doesn't require sacrificing their own passion for life. And it will benefit your marriage by strengthening your bond, and reaffirming your commitment to each other's growth and happiness. Fan your partner's flames, and you might just be surprised how much fire they have within them.

A few years ago, Sarah worked for the state doing computer art. The pay was decent, the stress was low, and she got paid holidays off. Overall, not bad. She worked in her tiny little office for over ten years, and knew exactly when she'd be eligible to retire.

She loved the job when she started it. She was fresh out of college and this was exactly what she'd gone to school for. It was a perfect fit, and it satisfied her for years. But as the seasons kept changing, Sarah was changing too.

Her heart was calling her back to what she first loved about art—being hands-on. In particular, painting. But she'd invested over ten years at her current job with the state. Besides, the insurance was good, and retirement was only twenty years away. Mired in routine and familiarity, she did what many of us do when our hearts gently tug us in another life direction. She ignored it.

That didn't work, though. It just caused her to feel disconnected. Irritated. Unhappy. She tried to soldier on, but it was affecting her mood and attitude. Not just at work, but at home too. Something had to give. One night—in a serious tone—she asked, "Can we talk?" I was ready to listen.

Sarah explained her situation. That she felt stifled by the job she once loved. Not because the job had changed, but because she had. She wasn't sure she could earn a living painting, but her current job was no longer fulfilling her, and she hated that. To complicate things, she felt guilty for even having such thoughts. She was conflicted. Caught between wanting more from life, yet not wanting to be greedy or selfish. On paper, our life was great. But inside, she felt the light of her individuality dimming.

As she talked, it became evident to me that she only had two choices here. Quit, or let those once cozy office walls close in on her like a tomb.

I felt terrible. She was giving all of herself as a wife and mother. But her professional dilemma had her forgoing her heart's calling. She was muting her painting talents, and trading away the most productive working years of her life, and for what? Health insurance and a retirement date twenty years away? Seeing her wrestle with her situation, my warrior energy kicked in.

There was no way I could encourage her to play life small and conservative when her heart was telling her to do otherwise. How could I consider myself a leader in my family if I didn't encourage her to run, full speed, after her wildest dreams? When we got married, she entrusted me with her life. Just like your partner has entrusted you with hers. As I listened, I could see the flame of Sarah's passion was flickering, threatening to go out. So, I did what any good partner would do. I poured gas on it.

I thanked her for sharing her truth with me. Gave her a giant hug (while also grabbing her booty...hey, I'm still a man), and then I ran through her track record of accomplishments to remind her just how much of a badass she is. I encouraged her to listen to her heart, and reassured her that me and kids had her back 100 percent. Ride or die. Her eyes were glassy with tears of appreciation. I'd heard her, and she felt valued, loved, and respected.

The creative energy in the house exploded that night. "Kids!" I yelled out. "What kind of art business can ya momma start!?" Sarah laughed tears. In an instant, Adrian and Cassidy were both shouting ideas. "Oh, like teaching an art camp?" one asked. "Or like, being an art teacher at school!?" the other piggybacked. We bounced around so many ideas I had to grab a sheet of paper to jot them all down. As Sarah talked about business ideas, the kids drew company logos with her initials in fat crayons and magic markers. The session lasted over an hour. The look of relief on Sarah's face fed my soul. I knew we were doing the right thing, no matter how it turned out. That night changed life for all of us.

Today, Sarah is the owner-operator of her own—very successful—mural and sign painting company. Her work is amazing, and she has quickly established herself as one of the top muralists in our area. Our entire family has been enriched and strengthened by her courageous decision to chase her dreams and listen to her heart.

This is the type of support healthy and happy couples need

to show for each other. Speak life into each other's dreams. Speak confidence into each other's doubts. Raise each other up and fan each other's flames.

THIS LOVE IS MATURE

It requires a certain level of maturity both to give and to receive the type of genuine love I'm describing here. So exercise caution. If you try to give this love to someone who doesn't respect it, or isn't mature enough to understand how valuable it is, you're only setting yourself up for heartache.

Giving your love to the wrong person sucks. It's like feeding lobster to a toddler. Toddlers don't want lobster. They can't appreciate it. They aren't ready for it yet. Toddlers want mac and cheese with hot dog slices in it. Give 'em lobster and they're liable to spit it out or throw it on the floor. Your love is lobster, not cut-up hot dogs. Only give it to someone mature enough to know the difference.

FIGHT FAIR

No matter how much you love your partner, conflict is inevitable. Stay together long enough, and you're gonna have a few fights. In order to keep your relationship safe and healthy, it's critical that you learn how to fight fair. Given the dangerous and toxic environment that many of us come from, learning how to fight fair is almost as important as learning how to love. Here are some fighting guidelines all couples should keep in mind when there's a problem that needs resolving.

The first thing to remember during a fight is that you love each other. You and your partner are a team. Don't see each other as enemies. See the problem as your shared enemy. Work to defeat the problem, not each other. Once you're fighting against each other, nobody wins.

A huge component to solid relationships is trust. Not just the trust of being faithful, but the trust of not hurting each other. If there's a conflict and one of you starts to finger-point, and fault-find, and attack the other, it erodes that trust. It eats away at the structural integrity of your relationship. Your home develops termites. And eventually, it falls.

However, if you stay awake—aware of yourself—and balanced in your golden zone, conflict in your relationship can actually bring you closer together. You're an alchemist now; you can turn lead into gold. If you remember to love each other (actions + intentions behind those actions), and you truly listen to each other (with the intent to understand), then you'll come out on the other side of any disagreement stronger than you went in. When that happens, the win is twofold. Not only do you solve the problem but you build deeper trust in each other, and develop an increased confidence in your ability to work through whatever challenges and obstacles you might face together. Here are three key rules to fight by. Follow them, and a rocky stretch of sea won't capsize your whole relationship.

1. **Do It Away from Kids:** Never argue, put each other down, or insult each other in front of your children. Even if you and the child's other parent aren't together. Never insult or be critical of the other parent in front of the child. Remember, how you act and what you say is creating their idea of "normal." You're setting the standard. You're a leader, act like it.

If you and your partner are able to talk through a difference of opinions in a healthy and respectful way, letting your children see that will help them develop their own conflict resolution skills. But if your relationship is not that evolved, and conflict between you and your partner comes with the risk of it devolving into a straight-up argument or a nasty exchange, then make sure you're alone when you do it. However, I strongly encourage you both to move into balance, and to establish a new normal in your communication patterns. Because your kids are listening, even when you think they aren't.

2. **Own Your Feelings:** When there's a conflict, learn to communicate what you're feeling without blaming your partner for it. Take responsibility for how YOU feel. It changes the entire dynamic of a confrontation. Saying, "I feel disrespected..." is much more effective than saying, "YOU'RE being disrespectful." One opens an avenue for dialogue, one shuts it down. It may seem small, but the difference is palpable, especially in tense moments.

   "I feel unappreciated..." is ownership of feelings. "YOU don't appreciate me" is accusatory. When you take ownership of your feelings, your partner doesn't have to play defense. This allows you both to focus on your unified goal of solving the problem. But if you pin your feelings on your partner, the blame game and fault-finding cycle spins around and around, and no one wins.

3. **Stick to the Topic:** In an argument with your partner, your attitude needs to be one of—how can we fix this issue? In order to accomplish that, it's important that you stick to the actual issue at hand. When you come from a dysfunctional

home, you may treat every single conflict as a must-win fight to the death. This isn't healthy, and your relationship won't survive it.

I've had to work on this a lot. Early in our marriage, if Sarah and I were fighting and I realized I was wrong, I would unconsciously pivot the argument to a different angle—or a different topic entirely—and find a way to establish a winning position again. It's embarrassing to admit, but it's true. The scariest part is that I didn't even realize I was doing it. But as I became more balanced in my primal energies, and more aware of myself, I was able to consciously create new responses to those situations. Now, if I'm wrong, or I've somehow negatively affected the balance in our home, I apologize, adjust my behavior, and keep it movin'. Problem solved. It sounds simple because it is simple. It just takes a little maturity, humility, and balance.

Another reason couples often get off topic during an argument is that they aren't being honest about why they're fighting in the first place. Relationships are layered with years of complex emotional history. That's why it's so important to establish healthy communicative patterns early. If not, unhealed wounds get buried, and express themselves in all sorts of ways that stress relationships. Sometimes years later. Next thing you know, she's crying because you put the spoons in the fork drawer, and you're irate because she drove your car and didn't put the seat back. When the real problem is, neither of you feel you're being heard in your relationship.

The last thing I'll say about staying on topic is, after you've solved an issue, move on. Genuinely resolve it, and then leave it for dead. Dredging up buried bones of problems long solved is another relationship killer. That usually results from trying to bury an issue before it's actually dead—which doesn't work either. Stick to the topic, fix the problem, and once it's resolved, leave it in the past.

4. **Never Be Violent:** I shouldn't have to say this, but just so we're clear, don't fucking hit each other. I doubt you'd be reading this book if you were that type of person, but I had to say it.

    Along those lines, fellas, don't physically intimidate her. Don't grab her. Don't shake her. Don't threaten her. Don't shout at her. Don't abuse her mentally, emotionally, or financially. Don't call her names. Don't insult her. Don't make cruel jokes at her expense. Don't demean her in any way, shape, or form. We may have seen it growing up, but that shit stops with us.

It may sound awkward, but I'm very proud of how Sarah and I handle conflict. We fight fair, which keeps our quarrels contained and manageable. We don't let small issues become big issues. And when there really is a big issue, we jump it! We tag team it, and beat up on it together, rather than beating up on each other.

PRIMAL ENERGY SEX

Ahh...the good part, sex! Satisfying sex is important in relationships. That said, it's up to you and your partner to determine what "satisfying" means for you. When it comes to sexual frequency and variety, people are as different in their ideas about what constitutes good sex as they are in their ideas about what constitutes good food. How much spice you use—and how often you eat—is totally up to you. Just make sure you communicate openly, honestly, and respectfully about the topic with your partner.

Regardless of your sexual taste, feeling satisfied is a big part of keeping your relationship healthy and happy. Staying balanced in your three primal energies will serve you well in all areas of your relationship, including in the bedroom. Here are some ways you can use each to find yourself in the golden zone of satisfying sex.

- **Warrior Sex:** Warrior energy is where your raw passion comes from. Your animalistic lust. Sex, at its core, is a very animalistic act. Think about it, you're climbing on each other, grinding on each other, exchanging bodily fluids. It doesn't get much more animalistic than that. To find your sexual golden zone, and to help your partner find theirs, you've got to embrace this aspect of sex. Be a warrior! Not a dud. Get up in there! It's only natural.

  I know some of you guys are gonna misread that last part as me saying, "Take her to pound town!" That's not the point I'm making. I'm saying pursue her, make her feel wanted and sought after. And when it goes down, focus your healthy warrior energy on satisfying her. Use it to give her pleasure, not just to take your own. Because selfish sex isn't good sex. It isn't healthy sex. And it certainly isn't satisfying for the other person. But when two people are tapped into their healthy warrior energy, and they're committed to giving each other immense satisfaction, the sex can't help but be fantastic.

- **Intellectual Sex:** A big part of sex takes place in the mind. This is true for everyone, but it's especially true for women. Fellas, this means you've got to master stimulating a woman's mind long before you try stimulating her body. Think about healthy sex in your relationship as a physical expression of the mental closeness you share. What things do you do to strengthen your mental bond with your partner? Do you make her feel safe and valued? Do you listen in a way that makes her feel heard? Do you express your desire for her through nonsexual contact like hand-holding, or resting your hand on her leg while you drive? Are you trustworthy? If you say you're going to handle a task or responsibility, can she count on you to come through? Do you take her feelings into account about things? Or tell her she's beautiful in front of the children? Do you commit loving acts with loving intentions? All these things influence her mental stimulation and directly relate to the quality (and frequency) of the sex you'll have.

One thing Sarah finds incredibly sexy is the way I play with—and care for—the kids.

I guess there's something about seeing the kids being treated well, laughing, safe and happy, loving their dad, that activates *her* warrior sexual energy! Talk about a win-win-win situation. I enjoy time with the kids. The kids enjoy time with me. Then later, Sarah and I enjoy each other. Balance is beautiful.

- **Spiritual Sex:** When treated with the proper respect, sex is the highest physical expression of love there is. It connects two people in the most intimate way possible. Use your healthy spiritual energy to honor your partner sexually. Not just during the act itself, but in everyday life as well. You can honor your partner's sexual significance by the way you look at her, or by the way you don't look at other women.

These small acts communicate that you see her as sexually attractive, but they also communicate that you see her as spiritually attractive. They let her know you desire her on every level. Feeling wanted and appreciated in this way not only fosters a healthy sexual energy between couples, but it adds a layer of spiritual divinity to it.

Apply these techniques, incorporate your warrior, intellectual, and spiritual energies into your sex life, and it'll take on a whole new level of gratification. For both of you. You'll be in the golden zone of good, meaningful, fulfilling sex.

HELP HER FIND HER GOLDEN ZONE

One way to lead in your marriage is by helping your partner find their own balanced golden zone. No person is responsible for creating another person's happiness. This includes husband and wife. If you think it's your spouse's responsibility to make you happy, you're both gonna be in for a rough ride. Happiness comes from within. Expecting someone else to provide it for you is immature.

However, you can—and should—help your partner find their balanced golden zone. Too often, relationships devolve into couples trying to control each other, manage each other, and limit each other's happiness. This is the complete opposite of healthy love. People in the strongest relationships understand that they don't own each other. Like Buddhist monk Thich

Nhat Hanh once said, "You must love in such a way that the person you love feels free."

While I can't control Sarah's happiness any more than she can control mine, I can work to make her feel free by helping her live in her golden zone. You should do the same for your spouse. Here are some examples how.

- **Her Warrior Energy:** What are some healthy ways your partner expresses their warrior energy? Sarah's got a lot of fighting spirit. Which I respect. These days, she channels most of it into running her business. Before that, she ran triathlons. Or worked out with friends, or ran obstacle courses with me. While her targets changed, her warrior energy has stayed consistent. I do my best to keep that spirit alive in her. While I'm not responsible for her happiness, I know letting her get off-balance will lead to her unhappiness. This means sometimes I have to take care of the kids alone for a few days while she's out of town painting. In the past it's meant taking care of home while she trains for races. It's even meant signing up for half-marathons myself (which isn't my thing) so that she and I could train and spend some time together.

  Ask yourself, what unique ways does your partner express their warrior energy, and are you helping to create guilt-free opportunities for them to do so? This attitude may just change the way you look at some of your spouse's activities and hobbies, and develop a new appreciation for them.

- **Her Intellectual Energy:** What does your partner like to do to stimulate their intellectual energy? How do you help them do it? Sarah loves the intellectual stimulation of traveling and experiencing different places, people, and cultures. She loves the process of planning and coordinating adventures for the whole family.

So, we travel! We have a giant map on the wall in our home. And we use it to look at the world. We've been to some pretty amazing places, and have a serious list of places we'd like to make it to one day. By researching potential adventures for us, not only does Sarah get her intellectual energy fed, but the kids do too. They're getting real-life experiences about the world that you can't learn in a classroom. Traveling provides them with character-shaping experiences that make fun and lasting memories for the whole family.

Again, there is no right or wrong here. What feeds your intellectual energy is right for you. I'm a reader. I love getting into good books. Sarah reads one page and falls asleep. It's actually a running joke in our house. It literally took her two years to work her way through one particular book. Now, imagine if I tried to stoke her intellectual energy by getting her a book that I like. Terrible idea! But that type of thing happens a lot in relationships. See your partner! Learn what speaks to them, and then help them get more of that in their lives. That's love.

· **Spiritual Energy:** Sarah gets her spiritual bucket filled through art. When she's painting, and she's locked into a project, the rest of the world melts away. She's at peace, her purpose flows through her, and she feels a deep sense of connection. Me, I suck at painting. The only thing it makes me feel is anxiety. So, it's not how I fill my bucket. But I certainly try to help Sarah create opportunities to fill hers.

Part of that means showing interest in what she's doing. It means helping in any way I can. Just being near her while she's so tapped in makes me feel good too.

So, what fills your partner's spiritual bucket? What makes them feel light and alive? Do you know? Whatever it is, you need to respect it. Because it gives your partner the vital spiritual energy they need to stay healthy and happy.

GET INTO THE GOLDEN ZONE

Warrior Energy: Channel your warrior energy appropriately. You're a strong fighter. Be sure you're fighting for—rather than against—your partner.

Intellectual Energy: Understand that loving your wife is a gift to your whole family. Loving her fully means helping her find her own golden zone. Support her in all her roles, not just as a wife and mother, but also as an individual.

Spiritual Energy: See the divinity in your union. Love your partner as you love yourself. View serving and exalting your partner as an honor, not an obligation.

The Golden Zone: Here, you and your spouse share an ever-growing, upward spiral of love and respect for each other. You communicate effectively and fight as a team to overcome challenges. You honor each other and prioritize your relationship. Your connection is tight mentally, physically, and spiritually. You're both strong on your own and even stronger together. Your children see the world as a safe and loving place based on the energy in your home. They have confidence that they can go out into it and do amazing things. The golden zone becomes their normal.

The Golden Zone:

- Fight Fair

- Love Her Wholly

- Connect on Every Level

CHAPTER 8

● ● ●

SON RISE: PARENTING YOUR SON FROM THE GOLDEN ZONE

So far in this book, I've focused on all the preparatory work necessary for being a first generation father. From learning the three primal energies, to healing old wounds, to understanding what healthy and happy love looks like. All of the personal development and growth you've done so far has been in preparation for this moment: being a parent.

In this chapter, I'll give you insightful, practical advice on how to parent your son from the golden zone. I'll cover what to expect as a first-time father, and things you can do to create a healthy and happy environment before your baby even arrives. We'll start there, and go all the way to helping your son develop traits of healthy masculinity, and finding his own golden zone.

Imagine how much strength, balance, and love your boy will be able to offer the world having been raised with full awareness and mastery of his three primal energies. Think of all the pain and anguish you'll be saving him by keeping him from having to learn everything the long and hard way, like we did. The lessons you'll be able to teach him—coupled with the example you'll be setting for him—are an invaluable gift. You're about to set your son up for the type of success fathers dream of for their children. Not only are you providing him with a healthy and happy home, but you're giving him the gift of understanding himself. You're giving him true freedom.

BABY ON THE WAY...

Even before your child arrives, you need to embrace the idea that leadership is service. One way you can be of service to your unborn son is by taking care of momma. This means being proactive and anticipating ways to help her. There are entire books dedicated to the topic of what pregnancy is like and what expecting fathers can do to make life easier for their partners. I'm not gonna make a long list. But here are the top three bits of insight I think every man should know about his pregnant partner. They helped me understand what Sarah was going through, and how I could make things easier for her before birth.

1. **Nesting:** Nesting is a strong natural instinct that compels expecting mothers to clean and organize. Especially in areas dedicated to the baby. During this phase, your woman may find herself feeling panicked, stressed, and underprepared. This is natural.

   Understanding what she's experiencing will serve both of you well. It'll give you insight into what she's thinking and feeling, and what's driving it. Use this insight to step your game up, and help alleviate her stress and anxiety. She's gonna have a sense of urgency about all baby-related tasks.

Understand that, and don't wait until the last minute to get things ready. Be proactive about stuff, and if you say you're going to do something—do it. Don't wait. This'll make her feel better and show her that you're as serious and focused on the upcoming responsibility of parenthood as she is.

2. **Fatigue:** She's gonna be tired. Which should go without saying, since she's got a whole person growing inside her! I'm tired after a big lunch, so imagine. Have some awareness. Let her rest as much as she needs to, and be proactive about finding ways to help her. Regardless of your living situation, don't make her ask you for help. You need to be asking for ways that *you* can help. There's no room for ego, or silly immaturity here. You're about to be a parent. If you've chosen a partner with high moral character, you don't need to worry about her manipulating you or taking advantage of your willingness to help. See helping your pregnant partner as much as you can for what it truly is: leadership.

   If you've already got a child and you're expecting another one, it's even more important that you ramp up your help. Keeping up with even the most well-behaved kiddos is exhausting. Make sure to run interference on your first child (or children) so that wifey can get her downtime here and there. It'll keep her from feeling exhausted, overwhelmed, and frustrated.

3. **Her Changing Body:** During pregnancy, a woman's body goes through significant physical and hormonal changes. Be mature enough to understand what's happening, and be patient and supportive as she adjusts. She may be moody or emotional. She may not want to have sex, or she may

want to have lots of sex! All of this is normal, and you need to maintain your balance in the golden zone regardless of how she's feeling on any particular day.

Here's a pro tip for you: after the baby is born, it's gonna take at least six months for her hormones to get back to normal. In that time, exercise the same amount of understanding and support as you did during the pregnancy stage. Don't think that immediately after delivery she's gonna look—or feel—like she did before she was pregnant. It takes time.

Here's another pro tip: if your pregnant wife wants sex, give it to her. If she puts in a service ticket, you're obligated to deliver. Here's why. If you turn her offer down, she won't just see you as rejecting sex, she'll see you as rejecting *her.* She's likely to assume you don't find her attractive anymore. She may wonder if you regret the baby already, or if you're thinking of other women. Has she lost her sexual appeal? Is it ever gonna come back? You turned down her request for intimacy while she was in her most vulnerable state? You bastard!

You may just be tired, or not in the mood for sex at that moment. That doesn't matter, champ. You're in the big leagues now. If she asks, access your warrior energy, and handle biz. You can do it.

BABY'S HERE!

Congratulations, it's a boy! I hope momma and baby are both doing well. You rush to the calendar to see when Little League All-Star tryouts are. Hmm...still years away. Now what? These early days and years as new parents are very trying. You'll both be tired. You'll both be stressed. You'll both feel like you're doing all you can, and that it's not enough. And, if you're like most people, you won't have enough money either. Are we having fun yet!? Don't worry, things *will* get better.

Get in There: For a lot of dads, the arrival of their baby is a bit of a letdown. Of course, society would never allow us to say this out loud. But the reality is, it can feel anticlimactic. If you have these feelings, don't panic. It doesn't mean you're not gonna be an awesome dad. It just means you're a real person. This is normal.

An even lesser talked about norm is that some women feel the same way. From subtle feelings of anxiety and mood swings—often referred to as the "baby blues," to more significant full-blown postpartum depression, it's common for women to feel a flurry of confusing and conflicting emotions in the time after birth. During these times, focus your warrior, intellectual, and spiritual energies on understanding her and helping her. Doing so will take a lot of pressure—and maybe even guilt—off your partner, and allow her to recover quicker.

Early on, your baby is in what I call the "sack-o-potatoes phase." They just kinda sit there. Besides crying and eating, they don't do much. It can seem like your involvement with the baby during this phase isn't important. But it's very important! Your son's brain is processing things at an unbelievable rate. It's learning to be a human. Your baby needs to see your face, and hear your voice, and feel your touch. He needs to make the connection, from his earliest formation of thoughts, that *you* are an ever-present, reliable, consistent source of love and safety in his life. And you can only do that by getting in there.

This means giving him undivided attention. It means getting down on the floor with him, talking to him, bathing him, changing him, soothing him when he's upset. It means letting him study your face and your different tones of voice. It means being Daddy.

Even if it seems like none of this is resonating with him, it is. You're helping create a map of the world in his mind. And on that map, you're marking yourself as "home." Every day, your son shapes the lens through which he sees the world. You need to be involved in the shaping of that lens. You do that by spending quality time with him, and you do it by making sure the energy in your home is balanced, healthy, and happy.

Show Affection: Affection and positive attention are like sunlight and water to our budding boys. They need it in order to grow. Sadly, many of us grew up without regular healthy affection from men, so we're uncomfortable with it. We've never learned loving, positive expression, especially in a father-son relationship. This is a cycle that you're gonna break.

In generations past, it was common for dads to be stoic and emotionally distant. To rarely hug their sons, or say "I love you." That's just how men were back then. But that approach to leading a family doesn't best serve the son, or the father. So, we're gonna do better.

Ours is a more informed and emotionally healthier generation of fathers. We understand what our fathers didn't—the golden zone. This allows us access to balance and healing that they didn't have. They weren't bad men per se, but they were very often limited in range and depth. Their own malformations prevented them from showing healthy, positive affection.

Your children need your affection, both physically and verbally. Withholding it from them hinders their development. So, hug your kids! *Especially* your sons! Tell 'em you love 'em, and that you're proud of 'em. Pat 'em on the back. Put your arm around 'em. Let them feel your support! These simple, but often over-looked, acts will help you raise balanced, healthy, and happy boys, who in turn become balanced, healthy, and happy men.

The Power of Play: From an early age, your son learns and shapes his world through play. Some of the most magical bonding experiences I've had with Adrian came as we played together. It's as true today as it was when he was a toddler. Sure, as he gets older the games change. But play is still an important part of our time together. It's fun, and it's a great way to influence his life in a positive way. I've become quite the ninja at sneaking in valuable life lessons during games.

When Adrian was really young, and I was struggling to dis-cover what it meant to be a first generation father, playing with him was therapeutic for me. It filled my spiritual bucket. It also taught me how to be in the moment. When your child plays, they are fully present in a way that we, as adults, rarely are. The adult world has pulled our minds in a thousand different directions at once. We're splintered, constantly distracted. But a child at play is fully immersed in the moment. It's a beautiful ability that life tends to squeeze out of us.

Playing with my son helped me regain a sense of balance in my primal energies that I couldn't have anticipated. Later, when I started exploring meditation, I made connections between the presence that meditation teaches and the natural pres-ence Adrian experienced during play. This is just one—of the many—times I've learned significant life lessons from one of my kids. I sat down to play with him, hoping to sneak him a lesson. And what do you know? The little guy snuck a lesson in on me! Man, everything really does connect.

It doesn't matter what stage of development your son is in. He might be a baby, or a teenager, or a father himself. Regardless, make time to play together. It opens the window to laughter, joy, and connecting. Go have fun.

TOYS

As parents who came from drama and dysfunction, sometimes our desire to do better by our own children comes out in flawed ways. Like thinking we need to buy our kids the fanciest toys. Or the most expensive educational gimmicks. If you don't already know, you'll soon find out, kids are expensive. And the marketers who target parents are smart. They know exactly what to say to get you spending.

(Commercial):

Announcer in Serious Voice: "Do you have a baby? Does that baby sometimes...cry? If so, you need Baby Blinky Talk! It teaches your baby to talk, with blinks!"

Proud Mother's Testimonial: "My baby used to only speak one language...*crying*. He cried when he was hungry, he cried when he needed changing, he cried when he was tired! It was so confusing! Now, thanks to Baby Blinky Talk, my baby has learned how to say forty-two different phrases, all with blinks!"

(Close-up on baby): *blink blink*

Mother: "He said he loves it!"

Other Paid Actor: "Wow! It's a miracle!"

Other Paid Actor: "Genius!"

Other Paid Actor: "Take our money!"

Announcer: "Baby Blinky Talk. Because crying...is torture."

*Available now for only three easy payments of $99.99!

Parents want to give their children advantages, I get it. But real advantages don't come in a gimmick or a pricy gadget. If you want to give your child the ultimate advantage, be involved. Be invested. Be present. Play. Listen. Care. Make up songs with them. Draw with them. Read them stories. Explain shit to them. Nothing beats that.

Me, Sarah, and the kids regularly laugh ourselves silly just screwing around, and being with each other. When you're balanced in your golden zone, you can turn almost anything into a great time. Kids, no matter what age, just want your attention, approval, and love. And those things are absolutely free.

Yeah, my kids have the popular video game system that yours probably do too. But the hardest they laugh is when we're all watching the cats do something silly. Or telling stories about what happened in our day. Or when some other unplanned, organic bit of magic happens. These are the little moments of perfection we want to provide for our children, where they're making deep connections and also having fun. And they don't cost a thing. The only limitation is, you can't schedule those moments. You can't force them. You've got to let them unfold organically. And be there when they do.

WHAT IS TOXIC MASCULINITY AND HOW DO WE AVOID IT?

The term "toxic masculinity" is popular these days. It's mired in controversy, and has opened the door for broader national discussions about the roles males play in society. It's left a lot of fathers wondering: what does it mean to be—and raise—a man in today's world?

Although the term sounds (and is) negative, toxic masculinity isn't an attack on men in general. It doesn't mean that being a man, or raising masculine boys, is bad. The term describes a very specific, unhealthy expression of masculinity. It's the male whose fragile identity and sense of self-worth are tied to overtly stereotypical ideas of machismo. It's what happens when men act like caricatures of men: cartoonish, oafish oversimplifications.

Toxic masculinity results from being off-balance in your three primal energies. Here are some quick examples.

- **Toxic Warrior:** Overly aggressive and too eager to fight.

- **Impotent Warrior:** Masking their wimpy warrior spirit by overcompensating.

- **Toxic Intellectual:** Trapped in a narrow understanding of what being a man is.

- **Impotent Intellectual:** Lacks interest in developing new, balanced ways of seeing.

- **Toxic Spiritual:** Believes it is their divine right to be a douchebag.

- **Impotent Spiritual:** Believes nothing matters, so *why not* be a douchebag?

The first step in keeping toxic masculinity from taking root in our sons is to keep it from taking root in ourselves. We lead by example. We get balanced in our golden zones, and let our sons see what that looks like. Day after day. Only then do we have the credibility to talk to anyone else about balance.

The next step in keeping toxic masculinity at bay is developing your son's character. It's raising him to be balanced in his own healthy primal energies. Finding positive avenues for him to express his warrior energy. Keeping him expanding and evolving mentally. And helping him keep his spiritual bucket full.

An important thing to keep in mind here is that people change. What makes your son feel balanced one year, may make him feel stymied and resentful the next. Balance is fluid, it shifts and moves. If your idea of what your son needs for balance becomes stagnant—and you try to freeze his needs into one moment in time—you won't be able to reach him when he changes and evolves.

This is why it's important to teach your son how to understand himself, and find his own balance. When we show our boys—through our leadership—exactly what healthy balance looks and feels like, they're able to self-correct as needed. Helping your son develop this level of awareness and self-understanding will set a course of success and health for his entire life. Think about how powerful that is.

When we give them this amount of balance, we open them up to experiencing their full range of human emotions. We raise young men who become leaders themselves, balanced in strength, honor, and integrity. When we raise them in the light of the golden zone, there is no darkness within them for toxicity to fester.

HOW HARD IS TOO HARD?

For all the above talk about raising balanced boys, there *is* a certain hardening—a toughening up—that is a rite of passage from boyhood to manhood. As fathers, it's our duty to help our sons transition from boys into strong men. If we don't, we're failing them.

There are lots of fathers who never went through this transition themselves. They never really became men. Now they're just boys in men's bodies. And when they try to lead a family of their own, they find out real quick just how unqualified they are for that type of leadership position.

As we're raising our sons, the question here becomes: how hard should we be on our boys? How hard is too hard?

A common mistake we make is being too hard on our boys too early. This is especially true of fathers who come from rough backgrounds. When you come from an environment where the weak are preyed upon, a caring father feels like he *must* remove all weakness and vulnerability from his son. In the father's mind, this is a matter of survival!

When Adrian was younger, I made this mistake myself. I remember looking at him—even when he was a baby—and wondering how I could best equip him for survival. The more I sized him up, the more I felt he didn't have any killer instinct in his eyes—and that I needed to get him some. I tried appealing to him on an animalistic level. I'd show him my teeth, and growl, and make menacing faces. Trying to teach him how to intimidate an enemy with a death stare. But *hims* was comfy in *hims* plush PAW Patrol jam-jams, feet just kickin' away, lips wet with slobber, worry-free. I told Sarah, "He's cute. But I don't think he'd make it in the wild." I had a lot to learn about balance.

Fathers who try too hard to toughen up their boys usually do more harm than good. A sad irony. A dad wants to harden his son so he's safe from bullies. But in the process, Dad becomes the bully. Don't do this. Don't treat your son poorly under the misguided notion that it will somehow prepare him for when the world treats him poorly. That's totally backward, and doesn't serve either of you. That used to be a part of the rite of passage into manhood. But not for us. We're parenting our sons with love—into their golden zones—and we're leading from the front.

Helping our boys find healthy and strong balance means giving them what they actually need, and not projecting our needs onto them. Think about the three primal energies, and ask yourself how you're helping your son grow strong in each.

Warrior Energy: What are some healthy ways your son expresses warrior energy? Is he committed to something with a determined and competitive spirit that you previously didn't see value in? Remember, there are lots of ways to express our healthy primal energies. They don't all look the same.

Adrian, for example, doesn't like baseball. But he has competed for, and won, several lead parts in theater performances. Although baseball and theater are very different, the same warrior energy that drove my success in baseball is driving his success in the other areas. As leaders, we've got to see these types of underlying connections.

Intellectual Energy: What stimulates your son mentally? What interests him? Once you know what it is, don't try to invalidate it or discredit it—just because it doesn't interest you. See it for what it is, a tool to expand his intellectual energy. It can also be an opportunity to bring you closer together. Ask him to explain the best parts of it. Ask him what he finds so interesting about it, then listen with the intent to understand.

As your son matures, let him express his ideas and thoughts about things without you always correcting him—or explaining why he's wrong. Let him see you stretching and expanding your own understanding of things. One great way to bond over intellectual growth is to learn new things together. This reinforces to your son that learning and growing is a lifelong activity. Not one that stops at adulthood.

Spiritual Energy: What fills your son's spiritual bucket? Again, it may be different than what fills yours. Do you provide him with regular access to what makes him feel whole and connected? You should, it's a vital part of our leadership role.

Adrian loves cats. They genuinely light up his spirit. Personally, they do nothin' for me. I would never own one myself. But, given how much they fill his bucket, we have two: Kit-Kat and Karma. He loves those damn cats.

I can't relate to how good they make him feel, to the sense of connection and balance they bring him. But I don't need to. They fill his bucket, and that's all that matters to me. As his father, helping him fill his bucket—fills my own. Everything connects.

SUMMARY

Raising our sons up to be well-balanced, well-adjusted men isn't easy. It requires a lot from us. Primarily, it requires that we're well-balanced and well-adjusted ourselves. Remember, loving our sons starts with loving their mother. Even if you're not together as a couple—you still need to treat your child's mother with dignity and respect, regardless of if you think she deserves it or not. See it as an act of healthy leadership for your child.

Through all the different stages of his development, your son needs positive affection from you. The way you express this affection may change over time, but the intent behind it should always remain the same: to communicate love. Be present in your son's life. Be there for him physically, mentally, and spiritually. If you are, you'll likely find that for all you teach your child about life—he'll teach you just as much in return. Being a father to a son is truly an amazing experience. One that I'm thankful for every day. There's only one other feeling in parenthood that can rival it.

CHAPTER 9

• • •

DADDY'S GIRL: PARENTING YOUR DAUGHTER FROM THE GOLDEN ZONE

There's just something special about raising little girls, about the father-daughter relationship. If you have a daughter, you know exactly what I mean. Of course, I love my son with all of my heart. But my daughter, Cassidy, and I share a unique bond. One that's unlike any other.

For lots of first generation fathers, it can feel intimidating and overwhelming trying to figure out what our daughters need from us. Many find raising boys to be easier. We were boys ourselves not long ago. We understand what boys need and how to prepare them for adult life as men. With daughters, though, things can be quite different. Figuring out how to best prepare our sweet little girls to survive—as women—in this crazy world can be scary and confusing.

In this chapter, I'll cover things that all dads of daughters should know, including tips that will help you meet your daughter's unique mental and emotional needs. Brace yourselves, dads. This means understanding the difference between masculine and feminine energy, and learning how to access both of those energies within ourselves. Don't panic, it's not as bad as you might think.

Daughters are amazing. While they are different from sons, your big-picture goal in raising both should be the same. To give them a healthy and happy home. To make them feel unconditionally loved and supported. And ultimately, to parent them into their own golden zones: balanced in their warrior, intellectual, and spiritual energies. Let's get to it.

CASSIDY VS. RED SHIRT

My daughter, Cassidy—we call her CJ—is the sweetest, funniest, no-nonsense little firecracker I've ever met. Not only is she smart and talented, but she's very much the glue that bonds our family together. One spring day we were all at the park, enjoying the sunshine and fresh air. Eventually, Cassidy and I wandered off on our own little adventure. We explored, played follow the leader, chased each other around, and laughed at our silliness. Days like that are the best.

One thing about CJ is that she's a fast runner! She can move. This makes me especially proud because I was one of the fastest kids in my neighborhood. When you grow up poor, being fast gets you respect. Even in my elementary school days—when I was a crossing guard and regularly made the honor roll—I got a pass with the tougher kids because I was fast.

My children are growing up in a different world. In their world, being a fast runner doesn't mean much. Still, when I see Cassidy hit the turbo boosters and dust some unsuspecting kid in a footrace, my public-school heart swells with pride.

As she and I enjoyed the day, three boys—all a little older than her—came out of nowhere. They were talking a little rougher than my own kids do. They weren't being disrespectful, but they were loud and a little edgy, especially in the way they joked with each other. I figured I'd give them some positive adult attention, and help channel their warrior energy into something fun, like a race! I playfully chided them.

"Hey, are any of y'all fast runners? Probably not. I'm lookin' for somebody to race, but I don't wanna hurt your feelings so, I'll probably just race my daughter here." They immediately took the bait.

"*What*, I'm fast! I'm prolly faster than you!"

I already had 'em.

I quickly organized several races, and the kids loved it. Of course, I delivered my hard-hitting dad commentary the whole time:

"Here we are, ladies and gentlemen, trying to determine who is the fastest young athlete in all of Central Texas. We're down to our four finalists: Purple Shorts Kid—who looks like a real speed demon. No Shirt—who's not weighed down by any upper body strength. Red Shirt—who may actually be a high schooler. And Cassidy! AKA CJ Bear! The cute assassin with curly hair!"

Kids eat this kind of attention up. It fills their spirit when adults focus their creative energy on them. These kids were no different. I didn't know them, but I was trying to create a scenario that brought some balance to their primal energies. There was the physical aspect of running and competing to feed their warrior energies. There were the rules, race structure, and commentary to spark their intellectual energy. And there was the sense of community and connection to feed their spiritual energy. When you're in your own golden zone, and you firmly understand the principles, you can help everyone around you work toward theirs too. Friends, family, coworkers, strangers.

After a few different races, it came down to Cassidy vs. Red Shirt for the championship.

"OK!" I called out. "This is for all the marbles!"

Cassidy had barely beaten two of the boys, but Red Shirt had demolished them. He was clearly the fastest kid, and his buddies were hyping him up. They needed him to beat CJ, and represent for the guys. For a silly little made-up event at the park, it was pretty intense!

Cassidy smiled sheepishly as the other boys hooted and hollered. I could tell she was a little intimidated. I just smiled back at her, and let her feel the weight of the situation. I didn't say a word.

"OK! LINE IT UP!" I commanded. And they did.

"RED SHIRT, READY!? CASSIDY, READY!? ON YOUR MARKS! GET SET! GO!!"

Red Shirt took off like a rocket! His buds cheering him on. CJ, on the other hand, kinda tip-toed out of the gate. Red Shirt ran as hard as he could. Cassidy ran just hard enough to make it look like she was trying. Red Shirt won easily. His boys celebrated. I saw what had happened and pulled Cassidy aside for a chat.

She had allowed herself to get psyched out. She'd convinced herself that she couldn't beat Red Shirt, nobody could! So, rather than try her absolute best, she gave it a half-hearted effort. Moments like this are why I love sports. There are so many valuable lessons we can learn and apply to everyday life. We've all psyched ourselves out of things, convinced ourselves we can't win, and then given less than our best effort. It happens every day. I bet you wouldn't have to think very long to find an example of how you're doing it with something in your life right now.

As first generation fathers, we've got to understand that when we try our absolute best at something, at anything, it has a positive effect on our families. As men raising daughters, it's critical we teach them it's OK to try their best! Sometimes the world guilts girls (and women) for trying to accomplish things. We need to teach our daughters not to succumb to such pressures. Teach them not to apologize for being amazing and successful. And most importantly, teach them not to accept anything less of themselves than their absolute best effort. When CJ and I got done talking, I called out, "REMATCH!"

Red Shirt didn't mind one bit. He was happy to race again. He never wanted the fun to end. This time when they lined up, Cassidy didn't look sheepish. She looked focused. I knew she wasn't gonna tip-toe out of the gate for this kid again.

I counted them down, and then..."GO!"

Cassidy jumped out front! Red Shirt, who had breezed to victory after victory, had gotten a little cocky. His eyes grew wide with surprise as the curly haired assassin blew past him. His smile melted away as he worked to close the gap. His neck started to strain. His face contorted with effort. CJ kept her eyes forward, focused, and ran like her life depended on it. Just before they crossed the finish line, Red Shirt pulled back in front, and edged her out.

"Oh my goodness, ladies and gentlemen!" I announced.

"What a race! CJ Bear vs. Red Shirt in a nail-biter! This was one for the ages as Red Shirt wins by a nose!"

Red Shirt tried to play it off like he knew he had it the whole time. But his weary smile said otherwise. CJ flashed me a proud grin. She'd lost, but she'd won. And we both understood that.

To help our daughters evolve into their fullest potential, we've got to encourage balanced growth in their three primal energies. Create opportunities, like I did in this race, for your daughter to learn, apply, and overcome. Don't let her shrink herself down to make others more comfortable. The world needs all that your daughter has to offer! But she can't unlock the very best of herself until she gets comfortable running with all her might.

ARE GIRLS AND BOYS REALLY DIFFERENT? MASCULINE VS. FEMININE ENERGY

As I've said, there are lots of different ways to be smart. One way I've had to smarten up in raising a daughter is by learning that there are feminine and masculine energies.

This was a major discovery for me. And learning how to consciously access both my feminine and masculine energies has made me a much better father and husband.

Before you freak out, the words "feminine" and "masculine" as I'm using them here don't refer to men and women. They have nothing to do with gender. They simply represent complementary expressions of the same energy.

Some may hear "feminine" and "masculine" and believe them to be opposites. I don't. I believe them to be complementary. The root word for "opposite" is "oppose," or to go against. Healthy masculine and feminine energies don't oppose each other; they complement each other. They enhance each other. If you want to access your full depth as a person—which your daughter needs you to do—you'll need access to both your masculine and feminine energies.

Again, *feminine and masculine energies don't mean man or woman!* Don't get hung up on that. Neither are bad, and both have times when they would be more ideal than the other. Here are some examples of each.

FEMININE ENERGY/MASCULINE ENERGY

- Nurturing/Risk Taking

- Intuitive Feeling/Logical Thought

- Creativity/Decisive Action

- Experiencing/Achieving

- Collaborative/Competitive

- Receiving/Giving

Looking at this short list, it's easy to see how the two different energies approach the same subject from complementary sides. Feelings vs. Logic, Competitive vs. Collaborative, etc. Why is this important to understand? Because to best serve our daughters, we need to be multidimensional. We need range. We can't pigeonhole ourselves into one narrow way of seeing and problem-solving. And we certainly won't understand our daughters if we do.

Effectively balancing yourself in your masculine and feminine energies doesn't mean being locked in 50/50 at all times. If you do that, you're cutting your abilities in half. Being balanced means having full access to either. It means being able to go 100 percent left, or 100 percent right depending on the situation. You can be all logic when need be, or all intuition. You can be all competitive, or all cooperative. You use your judgment to control the dial, making conscious decisions about how to best meet your daughter's needs in her life.

Understanding this allows you to access your highest potential as a first generation father. Being able to *range* into healthy feminine energies helps you raise your daughter, but it will also help your relationships with your son and wife too. The more tools and techniques you have at your disposal to build strong relationships with the people you love, the better you'll be able to lead them and serve them.

DAUGHTERS WITHOUT DADS

In the last chapter, I talked about the importance of being there for our sons in order to break the cycle of trauma and dysfunction in homes. Too often, though, the effects of absentee—or bad—fathers is measured only by how it scars our sons. But our daughters scar too. Our girls are every bit as devastated when they grow up without a positive father figure in the home. And they grow up to become women with their own unhealed wounds and malformations.

Young girls who grow up without loving and balanced fathers in their lives can develop their own unhealthy ways of dealing with that pain. Unfamiliar with what healthy male love should look like and feel like, they can find themselves in very unloving situations. They're often exploited, mistreated, and taken advantage of.

Their father's absence cuts two ways. It leaves them with a painful vacancy in their heart, and it also leaves them less wise to the ways of the world. Not only are the daughters traumatized by dad's absence, but they're also less prepared to protect themselves from people who would exploit that traumatization. A lot of wounded young women have had to learn some very hard lessons this way—being taken advantage of before they had a chance to heal themselves. As a result, a good number of them become single mothers themselves. Hoping, somehow, to find a way to break the cycle for their own child.

This circles back to the importance of loving your wife and how critical that is for your child's well-being. Letting your daughter see—day in and day out—what a healthy love looks like will set her expectations there. And when she's at the dating age, she won't accept anything less. If you and your daughter's mother aren't together, it's even more important that you treat her mother with decency and respect. This is serious shit. There's no room for pettiness or immaturity. Your children are depending on you.

ANYTHING *HE* CAN DO...

Your daughter needs to feel she has the same opportunities—and support—to achieve her dreams as your son does. Sometimes, as men, we're biased about what we think "girls" can accomplish. These biases can run so deep that we don't even know they're there. Those are the most dangerous ones, as they can subconsciously cause us to limit our own children. When we have different expectations about what our sons and daughters are capable of, our daughters notice. When we talk about their futures and what they'll go on to accomplish in different ways, our daughters notice. When we do these things, we say—without realizing it—that we don't think our daughters are as capable as our sons. And they notice.

We have to wake all the way up. We have to shine the light of self-awareness on these hidden biases, lest we inadvertently relegate our daughters to lesser goals and dreams than our sons. Which is unacceptable. We have to advocate *for* our daughters, not reinforce the glass ceiling that society would already put on them. You are a little girl's father. YOU shape her truth. Don't plant the toxic seeds of low expectations in her brilliant mind. From education, to extracurricular participation, to career options, to business ownership, encourage your daughter to become the very best of herself. And don't let her think for one second that her aspirations should be lower because she's a young woman.

SUPPORT HER PATH

A friend of mine recently asked how I would feel if Cassidy grew up to be a stay-at-home mom and a housewife. I gave my honest answer.

> "My job is to raise Cassidy to be confident and true to herself. If she's pursuing something that makes her genuinely happy and fulfilled, then I support it. It doesn't matter to me if she's a stay-at-home mom or an astronaut. What matters to me is that she has the courage to pursue what's in her heart—regardless of how others may look at her. If she's brave enough to do that, then I've done my job as her father."

As parents, it's natural to dream of the stars for our children. It's also natural to feel a sense of pride when our children accomplish something of significance. There's nothing wrong with that. But there is an inherent danger when you tie your own ego to your child's worldly accomplishments. When that happens, your children's lives aren't about them, they're about you. I'm sure you've seen mothers and fathers both fall into this self-centered way of seeing. It's unhealthy and uncomfortable for the child. And as these children grow up, they tend to distance themselves from their self-absorbed parents.

Our children's lives are not ours to own, especially as they grow closer to adulthood. My role as Cassidy's father is to get her so centered in her own golden zone, so locked into her understanding of high character, that her sense of self-worth isn't determined by any man's approval. Not even mine.

Here are some ways I make sure CJ is getting the balance she needs to live in her golden zone.

Her Warrior Spirit: Encourage your daughter to fight for what she believes in. Teach her to set goals, persevere, and to get comfortable trying her best. Protect her from harm, but don't coddle her from healthy challenges that will build strength and character.

Her Intellectual Energy: Recognize the brilliance of your daughter's intellectual energy, even if it expresses itself differently than yours. For example, while Adrian and I share a love of books, Cassidy's intellectual energy is expressed more in her passion for design and art. So, I make sure to encourage that, and I spend time doing those types of activities with her. Embarrassingly enough, her understanding of artistic spacing, composition, and color design is already ahead of mine—and has been since about the third grade.

A toxic father might try to discredit that and put a frustrating math problem in front of her. Instead, I encourage her to keep growing and expanding in her strengths. I spend time drawing and coloring with her. Watering her natural intellectual talents. Then, when it's time to do the mandatory school stuff—

reading, math, etc.—her confidence is high. Even when she doesn't understand concepts as quickly as she'd like, she never feels dumb. She understands that she's brilliant in her own way, and she's got a healthy enough warrior spirit to power through scholastic challenges. What piques your daughter's intellectual energy? Whatever it is, make sure you're carving out dedicated time to do that with her.

Her Spiritual Energy: What fills your daughter's bucket? If you honestly don't know, don't beat yourself up over it. That won't help. Just move forward from where you are now, with a commitment to understanding how you can help facilitate her getting the spiritual nourishment she needs—the type that lifts her up and speaks to her soul.

Cassidy fills her bucket with family time. She's lifted up when we're all together—eating together, playing together, sharing experiences together. Sarah and I are both aware of this, and make sure to get her the family activities she needs to keep balanced in her healthy spiritual energy.

SUMMARY

Your daughter needs you. She needs you to love and support her, and she needs you to love and support her mother. She needs you to set the standard for what a man should be in her life. Don't blow it.

Being the complete father your daughter needs requires balance in your three primal energies. It also requires having access to your full complement of feminine and masculine energies. Balance equals strength. To be strong for our daughters, we've got to be balanced. To help our daughters become strong themselves, we've got to help them balance. Everything connects.

Our children's needs will change over time. In order to meet them, we've got to stay observant and flexible. It's sad when well-meaning parents get stuck in a rigid idea of their child, and are left clinging to a version of them that no longer exists as the child evolves. Don't fall into that rut.

Your daughter is gonna grow in every direction. Which is great! Let her blossom into her fullest self. But she needs you to grow with her and to encourage her in both your words and your actions. This will allow you to gently and lovingly help her find her way into her golden zone and to stay there.

• • •

CHAPTER 10

THE ART OF DISCIPLINE: PROVIDING THE LOVING DISCIPLINE YOUR CHILDREN NEED

One of your most important duties as a first generation father is learning how to lovingly discipline your children. For many of us, the scars and malformations we suffered in our youth rear their ugly heads when it's time for us to be the disciplinarians. When we're acting from unhealed places within ourselves, we're in no state to administer loving discipline. In fact, trying to discipline your children when you, yourself, are out of balance can have disastrous consequences.

In this chapter, I'll explain the idea of loving discipline. I'll give you practical examples of how it should be administered, and I'll highlight some negative disciplinary traps that you must avoid. In order to give your children the type of discipline that corrects them, while also building them up and encouraging them, you need to be in your golden zone. Moreover, you've got to fully understand what you're trying to accomplish with your discipline. Only then can you figure out which techniques and methods will work best for you.

WHAT'S THE POINT?

The first step in effective discipline is understanding *why* you're disciplining your child. What's the point? What are you hoping to accomplish? If your "why" is *because these kids need they ass beat!* that's the wrong answer, Bernie Mac. Go to the back of the class.

If your disciplinary reasons are to change your child's behavior, you're getting warmer. Changed behavior isn't the wrong answer, it's just not the complete answer. OK, so what should be the point of discipline?

The point—the goal—the desired end state of any discipline we give our children must always be to bring them to a place of deeper understanding. And, no—*they understand I'll whoop that ass if they keep it up!* is not the type of understanding I'm talking about.

We want our children to understand right from wrong. To understand that their actions and words have real consequences. To understand the importance of showing others—and themselves—respect. And to understand that we're raising them to be balanced and principled. When they act in a way that goes against that understanding, our job is to help get them back on track.

This is very different than viewing discipline as simply punishing your child. If you discipline your child with the intent to *punish*, you both lose. Many of us grew up like this, with discipline that was intended to hurt us. It was punitive, sometimes even retaliatory. We've got to break this cycle, and elevate our understanding of discipline to the next level.

Before we can effectively discipline a child, we've got to make sure we're disciplined ourselves. So govern your intentions. Understand what's driving you. Never discipline from an angry or triggered state. If you do, it's likely to go wrong and backfire in the long run.

It's your responsibility to figure out what your child responds best to. Getting through to your child is a lot like coaching. The best coaches know each player is different. Some players respond better to being challenged, while others respond better to encouragement. It's the same with disciplining children. Some respond best to a loving explanation of why their behavior must change, while others need the volume of the message turned up a bit. It's our job to figure out what our child needs in any particular instance and then provide it. Even if it means gettin' a little dirty.

SMOKIN' THAT BOY

Adrian's always been a smart kid. Near the end of one school year, Sarah and I got a very uncharacteristic email from his teacher. It explained that he'd been throwing stuff in class recently, and his teacher wanted us to know.

We didn't panic or overreact. We did, however, have a talk with him. We asked him about it and listened as he explained his side of the story. It sounded like typical kid behavior, no big deal. His actions weren't being driven by an underlying issue.

He was just a smart kid, kinda bored in school, toward the end of the year, doing what he felt other kids were getting away with too. We understood. But we also made sure *he* understood such behavior was disruptive to the class, disrespectful to the teacher, and would not be tolerated. He said he got it, and that was that.

Shortly thereafter, we got another email from his school. Yep, he was throwing paper in class again. It was time to turn up the volume on my message. Not because I was "mad," but because I needed him to understand that this behavior was unacceptable. It distracts and disturbs the other kids, and it's an inaccurate representation of his character. At that point, if I didn't find a way to help him understand, I'd have been failing in my disciplinary duties. So here's what I did.

The next morning, I flipped his bedroom lights on at 5:30 a.m. and tossed him some gym shorts. "Get up, son. C'mon, let's go, hurry up! Put this on!"

He shot up, confused for a second, then got dressed reflexively. I saw him glance out the window; it was still dark outside.

"Wha...what are we doing?" he asked.

"C'mon, let's go. Downstairs. Put your shoes on! I'll tell you outside."

Once we were outside, I had his full attention. I told him that we'd gotten another email from his teacher. I asked if he'd been throwing stuff in class again. He started to offer an excuse, then caught himself. I was actually quite proud of that. I told him I wasn't mad at him, but that I needed him to understand that his behavior was unacceptable. And since our subtler conversation earlier didn't resonate with him, I was going to convey the message a little differently this time. Then it started to rain. Perfect.

I had him jog to the local park, about a quarter of a mile up the road. Once we were there, I gave him a good ole military training session. Push-ups, sit-ups, jumping jacks, log rolls, sprints. He was in elementary school, so I didn't have him doing anything crazy or dangerous, but I definitely had his attention.

Again, my goal here was never to hurt or embarrass him. It was to bring him to a place of understanding. Between exercise drills, I reinforced why his behavior was disrespectful to others, but primarily to himself. Once again, he said he understood. This time, I believed him. Afterward, I hugged him and told him I was proud of him. Then he jogged home.

He took a nice warm shower, and I made a big breakfast. As we ate, I complimented him on how strong he'd gotten. I told him a few stories about how the army would train us with the very same exercises he'd just done. I could see him making the prideful connection in his mind, *I'm as strong as a soldier!*

By the time Cassidy came downstairs, all sleepy-eyed, Adrian had already turned the eventful morning into a source of pride. He bragged about how many push-ups he'd done, and how it was raining, and how muddy he got, but how he didn't quit. This incident helped me understand the benefit of balanced discipline. It allowed me to turn a negative situation into a positive. It actually boosted Adrian's confidence and made him feel stronger and more capable. It became a bonding experience between him and me that strengthened our relationship. And it also served its ultimate goal, which was to help him understand that his behavior needed to change. It didn't matter if other kids were throwing stuff and getting away with it. He had a new, higher standard of personal accountability for himself. We'd taken lead and turned it into gold.

I encourage you to spend some time thinking about what discipline means to you. Are you disciplining your child with love? Remember, love equals action plus the intention behind the action. The goal is to bring your child to a place of understanding, and discipline rooted in anger and vindictiveness can never really instill a positive understanding in your child's life.

Which leads to the logical question.

TO SPANK OR NOT TO SPANK?

Spanking is a hotly debated topic these days. General public opinion is changing. We're moving from a society where spanking was not only common, but expected, to a society where spanking your child may get the cops called on you. Which team are you on: Team Spank? Or Team No Spank?

I've spanked both of my children. I don't spank them now, but I have in the past. Now, they're older, and mature enough to understand logic and reason. But they have each been spanked a time or two in their lives.

By "spank," I mean an open-handed, single swat across the bottom of the butt. I know that just hearing that word makes some folks cringe. If you're one of those people, please don't email me articles about how spanking traumatizes children and puts them on the fast track to prison. I've seen the studies. Hell, I worked in a pediatric hospital for years.

I'm not advocating for you to spank your children. But the reality is, I know some of you are going to. It's your family and your call. But if you do, please keep the points from this chapter in mind. Because the last thing you want to do is scar your own children, and pass down the trauma we're working so hard to fix within ourselves.

Swatting Guidelines:

- Never spank your child out of a knee-jerk reaction. That's unfair to the child. Spanking should only ever be used as a last resort, not a first response. Immediately resorting to spanking raises general anxiety in your child. It makes the child feel that although everything is fine right this second, they could be getting spanked at any moment. Don't do that.

- Swats should always come as the predetermined consequence for repeated, unacceptable behavior. In the very few times I've spanked my children, the consequences were always clearly outlined beforehand. I'd say, "I've already asked you not to do that. Here's why. Now I'm telling you, don't do that again. Here are some other things you *can* do instead. If you choose to do the other thing anyway, you're gonna get a swat on the butt. Do you understand?"

Clearly laying out the situation like this takes all the guesswork out of the child's mind. My kids have never had to worry about me flying off the handle and spanking them out of nowhere. Neither should yours. The few times young Adrian or Cassidy actually got the swat, they knew it was coming, and they knew that they'd earned it.

The authority to spank your child isn't something you should take lightly. It's not a tool that parents *must* use to raise healthy and happy children. Plenty of well-disciplined children have never been spanked once. A counterpoint to that is: plenty of well-adjusted, perfectly happy and highly accomplished folks were spanked as kids. The choice is yours, just make sure you're acting responsibly and from your own golden zone. But no matter which disciplinary tactics you find most effective, one thing is certain. If you say you're gonna do somethin', you better do it.

THE BIGGEST DISCIPLINARY MISTAKE

One of the biggest disciplinary mistakes parents make is the empty threat. You've seen it. The parent says, "Timmy, throw one more rock and we're leaving this park!"

What's Timmy do? He tests the boundaries. He throws another rock.

At this point, the parent has only one acceptable course of action. Pack up and leave. If they do, it reinforces in little Timmy's mind that when the parent says something, they mean it. It can't matter how much he protests or promises not to do it again. The parent has outlined consequences for a specific action and needs to enforce those consequences.

Have you ever seen a parent fold in a situation like that? It's hard to watch, isn't it? It just feels wrong. They tell little

Timmy throw one more rock and they're leaving. And, he does. Then the parent starts backtracking and changing their appeal to him.

"Timmy, do you want ice cream later or not? Because you're not gonna get ice cream if you keep it up."

Ugh. Terrible.

In this example, the child is young. But regardless of how old your child is, it's critical that when you state a fair and measured consequence for certain behavior, you follow through. By doing so, you make your child's world concrete and predictable. And you make yourself reliable and trustworthy in their eyes.

On the contrary, when you set a boundary for your child, then fail to enforce it, you hurt that child in several ways. Here are some:

- You undermine your own authority. If your child doesn't have to listen to you now, why would they listen to you later? You're setting the standard that your word means nothing. This has created a lot of little monsters who eventually grow up to become big monsters.

- It confuses the child. Your child needs consistency and predictability from you. If you're not upholding the boundaries you set, it creates terribly misbehaved children. They can never be sure which boundaries are real—and will be enforced—and which boundaries are flimsy and meaningless. These kids go through life testing the boundaries everywhere they go. And when a boundary is enforced, they often feel like they're being victimized.

- Ironically, your failure to follow through makes your child question even the positive things you tell them. The child wonders if your words of affirmation and positive encouragement are as meaningless as the boundaries you set. If the limitations you set don't mean much, your praise won't either.

Kids need and want healthy boundaries, routines, and consistency—even when they pretend like they don't. If you say it, you better be prepared to do it. Consistently keep your word, and your children will respect you more and test you less.

ANOTHER BIG MISTAKE

Another disciplinary mistake that comes from being out of balance is the overreaction. Oftentimes the empty threat leads to an overreaction. Have you ever seen this scenario?

A parent sets a boundary. "Do that again, and ___ will happen!"

The kid tests the boundary, the parent folds. This happens time after time, building up frustration and anger in the parent. One day, the kid does something that's not terrible by their own standard of behavior, and the parent snaps. They lose it. They hit their tipping point and blow up. In that moment, that parent is way out of control. They're out of balance, and in no position to administer healthy discipline.

See how these things connect? By failing to uphold their word early, this parent set the child up for failure, and set themselves up for frustration. This is why balance is so important. With healthy warrior, intellectual, and spiritual energies, you can discipline your child with firmness, with a deep understanding of what you're doing, and with the love. You discipline from the golden zone.

COMMAND TEAM

When it comes to discipline, you and your partner must have a unified front. You've got to be on the same page and support each other's decisions. Even if you and your partner disagree on how to handle a situation, support each other in front the kids, then discuss it privately. Never undermine or question the other parent's authority in front of the children. Never let the kids play one parent against the other. Even if you (the parents) aren't together anymore. These are *terrible* parenting mistakes, and they always end up hurting the child.

Sarah and I are one voice to our kids. When either of us says something, it comes from both of us. The last thing you want to do is create an environment where your kids only have to listen to one parent. Or where they're getting inconsistent messaging and conflicting instructions. You owe your kids better than that. You've worked so hard to establish a healthy, balanced home. Don't undo it all by undermining each other or letting the kids see you as anything other than a unified front.

In our house, this means Sarah and I present the kids with any final decisions we've come to as *our* decision. And it is our decision. We'll have already had our private conversation and come to an agreement. There is never a good guy and a bad guy, the decisions are always ours. In order to do this, it's important to avoid any sort of passive aggressive language that indicates that you don't agree. That's chickenshit. Remember, you're a team! Never scapegoat the other parent. I cannot stress that enough to both men and women. You might think it wins you favor for your child to see you as the "good guy." But that's selfish and deprives your child of what they need most, which is a mom and dad who are fully on the same parental page. So get there and stay there.

USE POSITIVE REINFORCEMENT

One powerful and healthy way to influence your child's behavior—regardless of age—is with positive reinforcement. This means noticing and calling attention to them when they're doing something right. Remember, the intention behind discipline is to help your children come to a place of deeper understanding of right and wrong. Therefore, discipline isn't just correcting your kids when they do something wrong. It's also encouraging them when they do something right. In my experience, positive reinforcement is one of the most effective methods of discipline. But it requires you being proactive. It requires you seeing the good your children do and putting a spotlight on it. An example from my home may sound like this:

> "Hey, Adrian. I heard you in the other room bein' nice to your sister. I really appreciate that. And you know it makes Cassidy feel good too. Great job, big bro!"

Or

> "Cassidy, thank you for doing such a great job of keeping your room clean! It feels so cozy and comfortable, I wanna sleep in here myself!"

When was the last time you praised your child for doing something right? A genuine compliment. Not the type with a backhanded insult tucked inside of it. You should be doing it regularly. You should be offering up the same level of daily appreciation of your spouse too, for that matter. A heartfelt, thankful recognition of someone's efforts goes way further in influencing their behavior than harping on the negatives. Plus, it allows *you* to feel good. I don't like having to come down on my kids. Encouraging them when they're doing the right things is much easier and feels better for the entire family.

Another thing to keep in mind about positive reinforcement is that children want attention. They want us to focus on them! If the only time you give your child your undivided attention is when they misbehave, you're ensuring that they'll misbehave. Ask any teacher, they'll tell you. The worst kids tend to act out because they really just want attention.

Nobody likes to be taken for granted. Children don't like it either. Don't take your child's good behavior for granted! Acknowledge it and call it out with the same energy you would bad behavior. Thank them for it! Show them that they don't need to act up in order for you to see them, and you might be surprised at how much they enjoy being well-behaved.

THE NO-BUT APOLOGY

Here's a transformative piece of wisdom that all first generation fathers must master: the *no-but* apology. This is simply an apology offered without qualifications. There's no "but" attached to it. It's, "I'm sorry." Full stop.

In dysfunctional homes, children are very rarely offered apologies. Even when they deserve them. And any apologies they do get are often just thinly veiled deflections of responsibility and shifting of blame. This creates a lack of trust and toxic relationships.

The no-but apology could have easily gone in the marriage chapter, as it's applicable there too. But I wanted it in the discipline chapter because learning to apologize to our children when they deserve it is a powerful way to break generational curses. I also wanted it here because the art of discipline isn't just about disciplining our kids. It's also about disciplining ourselves.

Being a parent is hard. You're gonna screw some stuff up. You owe it to your kids to have integrity about it. When you're in the wrong, own it, and apologize—no buts. Remember, your children are watching and learning from you. How you conduct yourself when you're wrong is eventually how they'll conduct themselves when they're wrong. Teach them, through your own actions, that recognizing your mistakes and genuinely apologizing for them is a sign of strength, not weakness. In doing so, you're giving them a gift that will help them in every relationship they'll have for the rest of their life. Some recent ways I've had to issue no-but apologies have sounded like:

"Adrian, I shouldn't have raised my voice. I'm sorry." No buts.

"Cassidy, the way I reacted was wrong. I'm sorry." No buts.

"Sarah, I had an attitude with you earlier, and I'm sorry." No buts.

"But" is a small word that does BIG damage to your apology. It undermines the whole thing. An "I'm sorry...BUT..." apology can do more harm than not apologizing at all. It's disingenuous and manipulative. Teach your child this lousy excuse for apologizing, and they'll eventually master their own double-talk manipulations. And worse, they'll never see when they're wrong, causing them to miss out on opportunities to grow and evolve. When you're sorry, say you're sorry, and mean it—no buts.

SUMMARY

Discipline, done right, is an art. But it takes discipline to give discipline. It's our responsibility to break the cycle of abuse disguised as "discipline." We do that by thinking of discipline not as a way to punish our children but as a loving way to bring them to a place of deeper understanding—and to facilitate their growth. If you come across internalized unhealed wounds while disciplining your children, you've got to do the necessary work to get yourself well.

Your child needs you to set healthy standards and limitations and to enforce them consistently. Your child needs you to be fair, and needs both parents to be 100 percent aligned in a unified front. No cracks. When you mess up yourself, apologize. No buts. Apply these principles consistently, and it won't be long until you find yourself in the disciplinary golden zone.

Warrior Energy: Check yourself, maintain your balance, and never discipline out of anger. Set healthy and consistent boundaries for your child and uphold them.

Intellectual Energy: Understand where your child is developmentally and research normal behavior (and misbehavior) for their age. There are normal brain development and hormonal patterns that drive our children to do certain things at certain ages. Understanding this will help put some of the things your child does into proper context.

Spiritual Energy: Discipline with love. It's an enormous responsibility to correct and discipline children in a way that serves them well. Don't take it lightly, and don't let your authority over your child corrupt you. Stay balanced in healthy spiritual energy and guide your children with a loving heart.

The Golden Zone:

- Be Disciplined Yourself

- Understand Them

- Help Them Understand Themselves

- Discipline with Love

CHAPTER 11

● ● ●

FIRST GENERATION FINANCES: HOW TO CONQUER THE POVERTY LOOP AND LEAD YOUR FAMILY INTO PROSPERITY

I come from humble beginnings. When I was in elementary school, my mom worked at a restaurant. She was a hard worker. But despite busting her ass, she barely made over $100 a week. Can you imagine raising a child on so little? No matter how lean things got, she did her best to shield me from feeling the financial pressures we were constantly under, but the struggle was real.

Part of that struggle meant being on welfare. I can assure you that "government cheese" isn't just a funny punchline about poverty. It was a very real thing the government gave out if you were poor enough. And we were. It was a massive hunk of rubbery yellow that came in a big cardboard box. And it tasted as good as it sounds. But hey, when you're in survival mode, you take whatever help you can get. I ate so many government grilled cheese sandwiches as a kid that I'm probably still digesting some now.

Even worse than the cheese were the food stamps. This was before EBT cards (which are used today) that you swipe like a credit card. I would have killed for that. Back then, there was no being discreet. Our food stamps came in thick paper booklets. They were like construction paper. Each denomination of bill was its own—attention drawing—color. The $1's were brown, the $5's were purple, the $10's were green. When you pulled out that big-ass book of Monopoly money, the whole store knew. I always felt like they were gonna make an overhead announcement:

(Bing) "Attention shoppers. Welfare check-out on register nine. Mixed kid with food stamps, register nine."

I would feel such anxiety and dread when my mom would send me to the corner store with a pocket full of stamps. I knew that if the wrong person saw me, the jokes would be relentless. I'd be dead. My tombstone would read, "Death by Food Stamp Roasting."

Looking back, I realize now that most of the kids in my neighborhood were poor. But there was such a negative stigma around it that we all hid our truth. This pattern follows many poor kids into their adult lives. It's a financial scar that keeps them trapped in poverty. It keeps them spending what little resources they do have on the illusion of not looking poor, rather than on trying to build actual wealth. It's a trap I've seen work too many times.

In this chapter, I'm gonna break down some of the ways poverty scars us, and how we can recover from its effects moving forward. It costs money to raise a family. Fair or not—the more safety, security, and opportunity you want to provide for your loved ones, the more it costs. In the pages that follow, I'll explain how I was able to beat the financial odds, and break the family cycle of poverty that plagues so many first generation fathers.

I should preface this chapter by clarifying that I am not a rich man—as far as money goes. So this chapter won't be about how to get filthy rich. But's that never been my goal. What I have done is: overcome the trauma of poverty, freed my own kids from its cyclical pull, and established a financially stable— and balanced—life for my family. Some would argue that *is* being rich.

RECOGNIZE THE CYCLE

Balance in your primal energies affects every aspect of your life, including finances. Think of poverty as an extreme imbalance in your relationship with money. As fathers, it's critical that we correct this imbalance, since poverty tends to be cyclical through generations. Growing up poor (and in dysfunction) limits a person's opportunities in life. Those limited opportunities create poor adults. Those poor adults go on to raise poor children. And the cycle starts all over again.

Unfortunately, poverty and broken homes are often joined at the hip. Meaning the person who suffered through one, often suffered through both. Everything connects. Many people never overcome this imbalance. They internalize it, and it becomes a permanent part of how they see themselves.

These people have untreated financial wounds. If they don't learn to heal them—and establish a healthy relationship with money—the families they're raising are likely to continue the poverty cycle.

So, how do we break it? How do we use our warrior, intellectual, and spiritual energies to get to a healthy place financially? In short, we do so by focusing our warrior energy on earning. We commit, and grind, and refuse to let our families suffer. We focus our intellectual energy on understanding money. A great way to increase your own understanding is through teaching. Teach your children the things you wish you'd learned early. Like how interest and credit works. Use your intellectual energy to establish realistic financial goals (such as saving 10 percent of your income—if not 10 percent, then 5 percent) and make actionable plans to achieve those goals. We focus our spiritual energy on making sure our financial pursuits are aligned with our values and principles. Also, we center ourselves in appreciation for all we do have, and all that's on the way. When the path we're on requires walking by faith, rather than walking by sight, it's our healthy spiritual energy that will see us through.

We don't all gotta be rich. But as parents, we've all got to establish a positive relationship with money. We've got to develop financial habits that allow us some breathing room. Building and maintaining a healthy and happy home is hard enough, but it's almost impossible when you're broke.

SHIFT YOUR MINDSET

One of the biggest obstacles that keeps people from achieving financial success is not understanding how closely tied together their thoughts and their money are. The way you think—and feel—about money has a direct impact on your ability to make it and keep it. In fact, one of the worst-kept secrets among the financially successful is that wealth starts in the mind.

I'm not speaking to you from some privileged, ideological bubble. I understand there are very real social and economic barriers designed to keep classes divided. Within our current system, the powers that be very much want to preserve their power and elite status. For them, part of that preservation includes keeping poor people poor. But—and this part is very important for you to understand—that can't matter. You can't care. You've got to destroy every excuse lurking in the back of your mind that limits your financial health and success. Fuck an excuse. We've got to do whatever it takes (legally) to provide our families with financial health. As a first generation father, you do what you gotta do.

DO WHAT YOU GOTTA DO

Most fathers—at some point or another—have to swallow their pride and take a job they aren't crazy about. Or work a shift that's less than ideal. For years, I worked an evening shift because it meant an extra $5K a year. Sarah and I agreed it made sense. Although it was less than perfect, I did it until I was able to work myself into a better situation somewhere else. The point is, in order to provide, you do what you gotta do. Sometimes you just have to dig deep, access your warrior energy, and grind it out for a period of time. When you find yourself in these situations, don't focus on how bad it sucks. Focus on your commitment to earn for your family. And keep in mind that no job is meaningless. There is nobility in *all* work.

Besides, as an alchemist you can turn your lead into gold by appreciating shitty work situations. If you look at it right, you might just find that the job you can't stand ends up driving you to discover your true life's calling.

When Adrian was born, I worked as a security guard in an office building. Not glorious. My duties included: walking around the parking lot to deter theft, helping managers get into locked rooms, and wrangling smokers into the designated smoking area. That was probably the most dangerous part. Nobody likes being messed with on their smoke break. The pay was $12 an hour, and came with lots of Top Flight Security jokes from the building's employees. Not exactly my dream job.

This experience was a great initiation into fatherhood. It taught me that doing the right thing for my family wasn't always gonna look sexy or cool. Sometimes, it's gonna make you look like a big wienie. That's part of the maturation process. Not caring what others think of you, and prioritizing your family's health and welfare. For years, every day I put on my polyester pants, and did what I had to do.

If you find yourself in a low-ranking position, stand tall knowing that your rank doesn't make you. Your title doesn't make you. Your income doesn't make you. It's your character that makes you. It's your commitment to your loved ones that makes you. Anybody who looks down on a person working a legit job because they think it's menial or trivial can fuck right off. Their opinion isn't of low importance, it's of *no* importance. You keep doin' what you gotta do.

JOIN THE TOP 10 PERCENT

I once heard the motivational speaker Jim Rohn say that 90 percent of people don't have their financial goals written down. He said the 10 percent of people who do take the time to set financial goals, and commit them to paper, tend to reach them. So when a person is struggling financially, it's almost never because they didn't hit their goals. It's because they didn't set any real goals in the first place! I found that to be powerful. I also found it to be humbling because, at the time, I didn't have a single financial goal written down. I didn't even know what one would look like. So I sat, and I thought. Eventually, I came up with a goal: double my income. I had no idea how I'd do it, but that didn't matter. I wrote it down, and entered the top 10 percent.

If I asked you right now, what are some of your financial goals, could you tell me? Could you show me where you've committed them to paper? If your answer is no, you've got some work to do. Having clearly identified financial goals gives your warrior energy something to focus on, a target to hit. It allows you to evolve out of the imbalance of simply surviving, into the golden zone of thriving.

At work, when I wasn't busy wrangling smokers, I was formulating a plan to double my income. Yeah, I may have been a lowly security guard, but I was a top 10 percenter, dammit! Just having a goal made me feel good. It gave me a sense of direction, and it gave me a challenge. The hunt was on.

I started doing research. I used the Bureau of Labor and Statistics' website to explore different career fields. It broke down how much jobs paid (on average), how much schooling they required, and how many jobs were available in each field. Then I made a personal list of things that were important to me in a new career. It included: helping others, working with people, making good money (2x my current $25K/year), being mentally challenging, and a few others. After lots of digging, I found a match. Not only did it meet all of my criteria, but there was a program for it at Austin Community College, just minutes away from my house! I had a target to aim for, Radiographic Technologist. I started the application process immediately.

Four years later, I'd done it. I'd become a licensed X-ray tech. It wasn't easy. There were unforeseen obstacles and challenges. Such as: due to the prerequisite requirements and lengthy application process, it took me four years to earn the two-year degree. Also, in that time, our family grew from three to four—as sweet little Cassidy came along. My mom and her husband moved in with us for a while. And so did my teenaged cousin. Because we were limited on space, this meant me, Sarah, two-year-old Adrian, and newborn Cassidy all shared one bedroom. Not exactly the ideal study environment. But I did what I had to do.

After graduation, I walked directly into a job. And sure enough, after tallying up all my pay opportunities, I had almost exactly doubled my income! Which was the goal I'd set for myself from the beginning. It felt surreal. It felt amazing. It felt like I'd cracked some sort of secret code on creating reality. My only problem was, I'd accomplished my only financial goal. I didn't have another one. Which meant I was no longer a top 10 percenter. Once the shock of what I was able to do wore off, I started working on some new ones.

I told this story because I want you to understand the importance of setting financial goals. Especially if you don't come from much. Doing so gives you a target to aim at, opens up your mind to ways of hitting it, and opens up your spirit to letting the target hit you.

I also want you to know that it's never too late to adjust your life's course. I earned that two-year degree when I was thirty-five years old. At thirty-one years old, when I started, I could have easily said I was too old to go back to school. But in my gut, I knew it was the right thing to do for myself, and for my family. When you're a first generation father, and you're doing this thing with no clear map, you may find yourself taking the long route sometimes. That's OK! Just keep moving forward. And keeping doing what you know is right in your gut and in your heart. The time is gonna pass by either way. If you feel called to make a move, don't let how long the road is deter you. Saddle up and ride. Besides, the journey is just as important as the destination.

There's a ton of sound financial advice out there. The basics are all very similar.

- Create a budget

- Live below your means

- Avoid debt

- Save (at least) 10 percent of your earnings

- Have three to six months' expenses in an emergency account

While this is all solid advice, it's pretty standard, and you can get it anywhere. You don't need to hear it from me. What I'm talking about is how to focus each primal energy to help you become balanced financially.

So far, I've addressed the importance of your warrior energy—commit to earning. And the importance of your intellectual energy—set financial goals. But for me, the real financial magic has happened with the incorporation of healthy spiritual energy.

GIVE TO GET

Money, as much as people covet it, is just energy. It's currency, sure. It has buying power, yes. But it's really just energy. And we all know how energy works: you get what you give. We readily accept this adage as truth when it comes to attitudes or karma, but when it comes to money—we tend to forget. In doing so, we end up working against ourselves. For a long time, I was trapped in that same limited way of thinking. Here's how.

While working for money, even though I was working hard, my intentions were to *get*. To get money, to get benefits, to get paid time off, to get a raise. Most people work with the same intentions—to get. Getting as much as you can while giving as little as you can is just good business, right? No. That's not right.

While our society may work like this, energy does not work like this. The universe doesn't work like this. As I matured spiritually, I came to understand that my "working to get" attitude toward money was going to keep me in a limited position. Since my energy was focused on how to "get" money, the universe matched it, and focused on "getting" money from me. Suffering from unhealed financial wounds, I was determined to hold onto my Crown Royal bag this time. I dug in harder and focused more on getting. Life responded in kind and pulled back equally as hard. I wanted to work less and make more money. My job wanted me to work more and make less money. I was getting exactly what I was giving. I had a fighting spirit about money, and the world obliged in providing me with that fight.

Tired of struggling financially, and feeling like every time we got ahead something pulled us right back down, it dawned on me: what if I shift my financial outlook? What if instead of trying to *get*, I looked for ways to *give*? I didn't realize it at the time, but I was about to stumble into the financial golden zone. I was about to balance in healthy spiritual financial energy and unlock unimaginable opportunities.

I took on a giving mentality. Not just with money—although I've given away thousands of dollars to friends and family in need—but in my attitude. I sought ways to be of service to people. I sought out problems I was uniquely qualified to help people solve. My attitude became, how can I GIVE to the world? What service can I provide that adds value to people's lives? This is the exact opposite of thinking, how can I *get* from the world? Do you see it?

One day, I was talking to a doctor I worked with, and I shared my revelation with him. He recommended I read a book called *The Go-Giver*. I ordered it that day. Its message confirmed exactly what I was feeling. That being of service to others, finding ways to give value, and being your authentic self while doing so, are key components to establishing real, transformative wealth. In other words, if everything connects—the surest way to get is by looking for your own unique way to give.

TEACH APPRECIATION

It's important that we provide our children with financially healthy lives and lots of opportunities. But it's equally important that we don't raise spoiled brats. There's something particularly gross and obnoxious about entitled kids. Maybe I'm still a little bitter about all that government grilled cheese. But whatever the reason, I cannot stand a spoiled child. I find it unbearably disrespectful.

I used to think anyone who came from money was spoiled. My understanding of the term has since evolved. Now I realize that having nice things doesn't make a child spoiled. What makes them spoiled is when they don't appreciate what they do have. When they take things for granted. When they expect to be pampered, catered to, and have an air of entitlement. That's what makes a child spoiled. And it stinks. You don't have to be rich to fall into this trap either. All you have to do is let your child's distasteful sense of privilege go unchecked. There are plenty of poor kids who are spoiled rotten too.

How do you find that balance of giving your child an amazing life, while also keeping them from getting spoiled? The answer is: appreciation. As parents, it's our responsibility to make sure we're teaching our children the art of appreciation. I know we want to give our kids the world. But we should only give them as much as they can appreciate. As much as they can handle without expectations or demands for more. Exceed that, and we're failing them. It's our duty to manage this. Not grandma's, or grandpa's, or auntie's, or uncle's. It's ours.

I'm incredibly proud of how appreciative both Adrian and Cassidy are. But it didn't just happen. Sarah and I are consciously raising them this way. They both understand that spoiled behavior will not be tolerated. They also know that if they're genuinely appreciative and considerate, we'll give them as much of the world as we can. Literally.

We teach our kids that the world is a big, beautiful, diverse place. We have a giant, high-gloss map in our home that we reference often. Earlier I mentioned that Sarah's intellectual energy is piqued by traveling and having new experiences. Those experiences cost. However, we've found some fun and creative ways to maximize our spending power and take the family out to see the world. Here's an example.

One summer, Sarah—before she started her own painting business—was teaching art to the kids. She'd gotten a big colorful book from the library that featured various artists. Every day they'd read about a particular artist, then do a small project emulating that artist's style. It was a great activity, and the kids loved it. They found themselves particularly drawn to the work of a Spanish architect named Antoni Gaudi. His famous buildings in Madrid attract thousands of people every year. Both kids built small clay structures fashioned in Gaudi's unique style, and they were eager to tell me all about him. They loved his work so much, one of them floated the idea of going to see some in person one day. The energy in those words hung in the air, and I could feel them wanting to come alive. By the end of the week, Sarah and I agreed, we were gonna find a way to go to Spain, and we were bringing the kids with us.

Now, an outsider might hear that I took my kids on an international vacation because they liked pictures they saw in a book and assume they're absurdly spoiled. But that couldn't be further from the truth. Sarah and I used this trip as an opportunity to teach our kids critical financial skills like budgeting, sacrifice, delayed gratification, and the importance of planning ahead, while also fostering a general spirit of appreciation.

The first thing we did was talk to them. We talked about how much money we made, and how much the trip would cost. We even showed them exactly how many hours we'd each have to work to pay for it. Their mouths about hit the floor.

Next, we put a fishbowl in the living room and called it The Spain Fund. We all agreed to prioritize saving. We weren't rich, so a trip like this—although possible—was going to require some sacrifices from everybody. Sarah is a phenomenal planner and got to work researching. She flexed her intellect, finding great deals, hidden values, when and where to go, and of course, kept the kids involved throughout it all. They had so much fun, and learned so much during their research, part of me was afraid the planning and anticipation would be more enjoyable for them than the actual trip.

We had a detailed spreadsheet on the refrigerator outlining costs. It would total over $5K.

This led to some great math exercises to figure out ways we could cut our spending, and put that money toward the trip. It was all done in a healthy spirit. Not to make the kids feel guilty at all, but to show them the reality of how much work it was gonna take to put a trip like this together. They learned a lot.

The best part was, they made financial sacrifices too. We'd let them make certain decisions for themselves, like, "OK, guys. We can all go to Dairy Queen and spend seven dollars a person. Or, we can put that twenty-eight dollars in The Spain Fund and make slushies at home."

"We can all go see the new animated movie, or we can put thirty dollars in The Spain Fund, make popcorn at home, and watch an old DVD."

The answer was always unanimous: "Spain Fund!" This went on for months. The more momentum we gained, the more ways we found to save money. I picked up extra shifts here or there—which suddenly wasn't a drag—since I knew the money was going to serve an amazing purpose. We stopped eating out. It's crazy how much dinner (plus a drink or two) can add up to over the course of several months.

Plus, when our families heard about what we were doing, they wanted to help out too! Sarah's parents contributed. My mom and her husband contributed. We didn't ask them to, but people like seeing others work toward a specific goal. Every time we'd saved enough money to pay for something, like the entrance fee to a particular museum in Barcelona, we crossed it off the spreadsheet and celebrated. In less than a year's time from when we first had the crazy idea, we did it. We flew the four of us to Spain for two weeks.

The trip was better than any of us imagined. It's a beautiful country, rich with history and culture. The experience of planning together, sacrificing together, saving together, and then achieving our goal—together—had a profound impact on all of us. And it left Adrian and Cassidy feeling the exact opposite of spoiled. It left them feeling deeply appreciative.

We've since used this same strategy to fund family trips to

China, Canada, and other cool places. And each time, we're appreciative of the opportunities and experiences. Appreciation is powerful. It turns lead into gold, and it keeps our children's hearts pure. Balance yourself in healthy spiritual energy, and you'll always find something to be appreciative for. Help your children find their way into their own golden zones, and their hearts will always be healthy, happy, and appreciative.

HAVE PURE INTENTIONS

It's great to establish financial goals and to work hard to accomplish them. But in doing so, make sure you're keeping your intentions—the reason you want money—pure. This will allow you to stay balanced in healthy spiritual energy as you meet and exceed your financial goals.

Like Jen Sincero says in her book *You Are a Badass at Making Money*, you can do so many great things—for yourself and for others—with money. You can enjoy time and shared experiences with loved ones. You can give amazing, thoughtful gifts. You can contribute to causes that you're passionate about. And for first generation fathers, having financial stability may bring a certain peace and security into your home and family that you've never experienced before. There's nothing wrong with having money. Just keep the reasons you want it pure. That way, when you get yours, you don't lose your balance.

WALK BY SPIRIT

On my path from security guard to X-ray tech, I relied heavily on my personal faith. I leaned on my belief that if I did the right thing, tried my absolute best, and followed my instincts, things would somehow work out. This meant a lot of moving forward with limited visibility. Walking on a path where I could only see two steps in front of me. On your journey, you're gonna have stretches with limited visibility too. We all do. As scary as it may be, we've got to keep moving forward. Stay balanced, stay principled, and when you can't walk by sight, keep your bucket full—and walk by spirit.

While I was applying for the radiography program, I was also working full time, taking prerequisite classes at night, and helping Sarah raise newborn Adrian. There were plenty of days when I felt overwhelmed and overextended. I know Sarah felt the same. She was working full time during the day, then coming home to care for Adrian alone while I was at night class. It was hard on both of us. We kept communication open, talked when we needed, expressed our doubts when we needed, confessed our fears when we needed, and expressed our anger when we needed. It wasn't always perfectly graceful, but we kept moving forward.

When I got accepted into the program, the celebration was short-lived. New obstacles popped up. The program suggested students not work. How could I not work? We needed the money. And if I worked, would I be able to successfully complete the program? The answer to all those concerns was the same: *I don't know.*

All I knew was, I was gonna keep walking. My gut told me the answers would present themselves when I needed them. In the meantime, just keep moving forward. Whenever I'd top off my spiritual bucket, I'd remember that it wasn't my responsibility to figure out every detail. My responsibility was to stay focused on advancing. It was to keep untying my own knots, and to keep working to find my golden zone. So that's what I did.

Sure enough, time after time, a way was made for me. A lucky break. A last-minute policy change that worked in my favor. Family generously offering help and support. I was even awarded a scholarship toward tuition. I was balanced in healthy spiritual energy—rooted in appreciation, and purpose, and faith. I was taking instructions from a higher part of myself. From a part *beyond* myself. A part that we all have access to when we quiet our minds and listen with our hearts. A part that has the ability to see us through anything if we just learn to let it.

GET INTO THE GOLDEN ZONE

Warrior Energy: Commit to earning—and saving—for your family.

Intellectual Energy: Identify negative thought patterns you have about money. Heal them by following them back to their roots. Spend time each day listening to or reading something positive about building wealth.

Spiritual Energy: See your spiritual health and your financial health as one. Find a unique way to give, serve, or solve problems for others, and you'll get in return. Both in financial rewards and in spiritual fulfillment.

The Golden Zone: Here is where all of your family's financial needs are met. You're safe, comfortable, and appreciative. You have a healthy relationship with money, and you're raising your children toward economic independence. Both your sons and your daughters.

You respect and appreciate money, but it doesn't control you. You don't work to get, you work to give. Ironically, this increases what you get tenfold. Everything connects. You're free to spend lots of quality time with the people you love. Your healthy finances are a reflection of your overall golden zone balance.

The Golden Zone:

- Commit to Earning

- Feed Your Mind and Set Goals

- Give to Get

CHAPTER 12

• • •

SLAYING DRAGONS: OVERCOMING FAMILY-CRUSHING ADDICTIONS AND VICES

I was forty years old before I was finally honest with myself about my drinking problem. I was out of balance. I drank every single night. Because I always handled my responsibilities, and because my drinking never led to any drama or issues in my home, it never raised any red flags. But deep down, I knew I had a problem. I also knew that if I didn't make a change, and find my balance soon, I would regret it. I grew up seeing the dragons of addiction and alcoholism up close. I knew the traumatizing effects they have on families and relationships. In my heart, I always knew that one day this dragon—this darkness—would come for me too. I thought I could stay ahead of it. I was wrong.

On your quest as a first generation father, it's likely that you'll find yourself face-to-face with your own dragon one day. Be prepared. These aren't obstacles that can be transformed into gold simply by changing the way you look at them. These dragons are ruthless. If you let them sink their teeth into you, they'll destroy everything you love with no remorse. They'll crush your relationships and ruin your life. I'm talking about the dragons of addiction—in all the various forms they come in.

Addiction is the compulsive drive to do something despite its harmful consequences. You know it's bad for you or your family. You know you shouldn't do it. But you can't *not* do it. That's addiction. And it's a monster.

While it's usually associated with drugs or alcohol, addiction can come in many different forms. It can be chemical or behavioral. Both can damage your family and cripple your abilities as a husband and father. Here are a few examples of each.

POPULAR CHEMICAL ADDICTIONS	POPULAR BEHAVIORAL ADDICTIONS
Drugs	Porn, Sex
Alcohol	Internet, Social Media, Video Games
Nicotine	Gambling

The dragons of addiction are master hunters. They're shape-shifters. They sniff out our unhealed wounds and prey on our weaknesses and unmet needs. No matter how well put together we may look on the outside, dragons aren't fooled by our masks. They will chase us forever. We can hide temporarily. But in the end, they always find us. The only way you can ever truly be safe from your dragon—whatever it may be—is to get into your golden zone and heal.

Once you're emotionally healed and balanced in healthy warrior, intellectual, and spiritual energy, you can fight your dragons—and win. But until then, neither you nor your family will ever be safe. You'll always be hunted.

In this chapter, I'll explain how to use your primal energies to defeat your dragons. And I'll share the details from some of my own battles. Some I've won, others I'm still fighting. Whether you're addicted to a substance or a behavior, if you're going to do what's best for your family, you've got to stop hiding, get balanced, and slay your dragon. So pick up your sword, my friend—danger lurks.

LAUGHING AT THE SKY

The sun felt gentle and forgiving on my face. Not angry and punishing, like the Texas sun usually is. I drew in a deep breath of cool air and exhaled slowly. I stood with my hands on my knees. Orange and yellow specks of light danced on my closed eyelids. I was floating. I had pulled my car onto the shoulder of the road, and trafficked whizzed by. People could see me, but I didn't care. The rhythmic tick-tick-ticking of my hazard lights sounded so balanced and predictable. That's what I wanted to be, balanced and predictable. But I felt like shit. I felt sick. I felt hungover. I felt normal.

I chuckled at my own pathetic state, then frowned at the taste of bile in my mouth. My abs were sore from retching so hard. But I wasn't done yet. Between hurls, I had a pang of clarity. I was out of balance. Despite the appearance of all being well, my dragon had sniffed me out. It also became clear to me that nobody would ever help me get my drinking under control. Nobody would even suspect I had a problem. I was too well trained. I could keep up the illusion until it killed me. And it was killing me. I felt another wave coming.

This one started deep in the middle of my body, as if my soul were trying to cleanse itself. Our bodies are incredibly intelligent. If we learn to listen, they'll very often tell us exactly what they need. Mine was telling me it needed to be reset. It needed balance. It was begging for it. I laughed, and surrendered to how I felt in the moment. I let it take me over, and I was thankful for it. Appreciative of it. I agreed. I would reset. I would go a full year without drinking. I would find my balance. With that, my core spasmed and clenched so hard it lifted me onto my tippy toes. This next year was gonna be a good year. I was already looking forward to it. Happy to be entering Day One. Although I must have looked insane to anyone passing by, puking my guts out on the side of the road, laughing at the sky.

WHAT CAUSES ADDICTION?

There are differing, and continually evolving, schools of thought on the root causes of addiction. Before I share my opinion, I should remind you that I am not a licensed drug and alcohol counselor. If you feel you need professional help, *please* seek it out! There are brilliant people who have dedicated their entire lives to studying addiction, and they can get you the help you need.

My interpretation of addiction is that it stems from simply not wanting to feel the way we feel. Maybe we're hurting, and we're trying to numb the pain. Maybe we're numb, and we're trying to feel something—anything. Maybe we're bored. Maybe the trauma we've experienced has made peace and quiet unbearable. Whatever it is we feel, we want to feel something different. So we make it different. We drink. We use drugs. We anesthetize our brains with hours of porn, or other mind-numbing bullshit. We overeat. We pound sugar. We lose ourselves in video games or in our online personas. We do all these things—even if they hurt us—to feel different. To get that little release of dopamine. And it works, for a second. But it's fleeting. And the next day, we feel even worse than we did the day before. Often ashamed and embarrassed. To cope with those feelings, we use even more. And that's how dragons are born.

DISCONNECTED: WHAT'S THE POINT?

Feeling disconnected from your life's purpose can also birth dragons. As human beings, we need to feel connected to something bigger than just ourselves. This is the crux of our spiritual energy. To connect us to purpose. A disconnected existence is hollow and painful. Without a sense of purpose, our wins feel empty and joyless, and our losses feel crushing. Our wins feel shallow to us because they aren't *our* wins. They're wins others say we should care about. And our losses sting twice as bad, since not only are we wasting our lives chasing other people's ideas of what matters—but then we lose on top of it. When this happens, it's easy to fall into hopelessness, wondering, *What's the point?*

Lots of first generation fathers don't get to see their children as often as they'd like, and it leaves a gaping void in their hearts. Society is quick to point out the stereotypical "dead-beat dad," but rarely talks about toxic mothers who use their children as a means to hurt a man. Who manipulate public sentiment and paint a picture that isn't consistent with reality. Who extort the fathers of their children for money. These women exist, and they leave a lot of frustrated fathers on the brink of some very dark places.

If you find yourself in a situation like this, it's critical that you keep your spiritual bucket topped off. You can't afford to fall into self-destructive patterns. I understand the urge to, but you can't. Your fight isn't done. Your obligation to your children isn't done. Consider it your obligation to your child to keep evolving, and becoming more balanced. To get healthy and heal.

Your child will come back into your life one day. It will likely happen with little warning or time to prepare. If you're all fucked up, it will only validate any negative thing the child's mother may have said about you. But if you're healthy and happy, balanced in your golden zone, and living as the best version of yourself possible, you will be in position to have an immediate positive impact in your child's life. No matter how long you were separated. I know this is the high road, and it can be tough to take. But it's what your children need from you. Even if they aren't in your life now, consider it your purpose to get ready for their inevitable return.

We all need connections. This is why groups are so powerful. From churches, to street gangs, to political parties, people need to feel connected to something. My purpose is to serve others. I serve my wife, I serve my children, I serve you. Think about it, I wrote this entire book in service to you. When you find yourself feeling disconnected and unfulfilled, find a way to be of service to someone else. It will add instant richness and meaning to your life.

FORGETTING WHAT'S UNDER THE MASK

We all wear masks to some degree. Polite society requires it. None of us get to go through life being totally, unapologetically ourselves. To navigate our way through the world, we have to play the game. We have to put on faces that don't always match how we feel. We have to hide our scars, bide our time, move strategically, and do what we have to do until we can do what we want to do. Wearing your mask well is part of being an adult. It's required for survival. However, it does come with risks.

The risk is forgetting who you are under the mask. It's playing your temporary role so well, that you forget it's temporary. It's losing your authenticity and losing yourself. Life's responsibilities, the demands of being a parent and spouse, can make you forget who you are under the mask. When you do that, it hurts. It more than hurts. It suffocates your soul. To ease that pain, people invite dragons into their lives. To avoid this common scenario, get back in touch with who you truly are. And never lose sight of that.

WE UNDERDOGS

The reality is, we're underdogs. The world thinks we're supposed to screw our lives up. Be addicts. Be poor. Have no morals. Leave our children fatherless and be a curse to the sad women who love us. But, fuck that. Embrace the underdog role. I've learned to love it! Not because I like playing from behind, but because it's the only role I've ever known. And I'm thankful for that.

We're all soldiers, fighting the same good fight. Healing, evolving, doing what's right. We're brothers, and I'm proud to be in the foxhole with you. Holding each other accountable. Not from a place of judgment or comparison, but from a place of mutual respect and wanting to see each other win. We underdogs, we gotta stick together.

For a long time, I fought my battles alone. I struggled in silence, too ashamed to admit when the complex issues I was dealing with were getting the best of me. Don't do that. Be smarter than I was. Use your warrior energy to fight against your dragons, not to hurt yourself. Use your intellectual energy to outsmart your problems, not to rationalize them. Use your spiritual energy to draw help from whatever higher powers you believe in, not to justify your broken human condition. And don't try to do it alone. Your ego may keep you from ever opening up, but that's poisonous. Find a friend you trust, someone who will listen without judging you, and talk to them. I've solved a lot of my life's problems by simply talking them through. Saying them out loud and breaking them down. If I'm ever in your area, I'd love to link up and hear your story. In the meanwhile, embrace the underdog role, and keep fighting the good fight.

DRAGONS IN DISGUISE

Addiction is most often associated with drugs or alcohol because they have the most visibly negative effects on our lives. But a person can be addicted to things that appear to be healthy or positive too. Like exercise or work. Anything you feel compelled to do, even though it pulls you out of balance and has a negative impact on you or your family, is an addiction.

A workaholic is seen as socially acceptable and almost praised in our society. But in reality, the person who uses work to hide from their feelings isn't healthy. And their relationships won't be either. Here's another example. Physical fitness is an important part of life. But the person who runs or works out excessively in order to avoid challenging and complicated relationship dynamics within their family only looks healthy. That's their mask. But in all actuality, they're off-balance. I've seen people's workout and training "schedule" wreak havoc on their relationships. A lot of times, those people don't even realize what they're doing. They're not aware enough to see themselves clearly. And while their actions may look healthy, they're not balanced enough to truly understand what's driving them. Which is not healthy. It doesn't matter what you use to avoid and distract yourself—might be crack, might be social media, might be runnin' marathons. If you're out of balance, and using it to escape reality, the damage caused is more similar than you might imagine.

MY DRY YEAR

To regain my own balance, I decided to go dry for a year. My drinking was never a threat to my family. I didn't act crazy or out of character when I drank. Still, it was robbing me of my life in a different, more subtle way. It was depleting my spirit. My energy was low, I wasn't as creative or alive. It was like I was in a constant, mild fog. When you're in this state, you're not sharp. You're not as vibrant. And you certainly can't be of genuine service to others.

Looking back on myself with nonjudgment and kindness, I see that I was under a tremendous amount of stress. I was trying to totally restructure my family cycle—with no roadmap. I was trying to identify deep, malformed wounds—heal them alone—while simultaneously raising a son and a daughter. AND trying to be of service to my wife, helping her come into her own self-actualization. I was working through generations of trauma and psychological PTSD. And I was doing it all while caring for sick and severely injured children every day. I was doing it! I was fighting the good fight, and I was winning! But it was a lot. And by the end of the day, I needed a drink. OK...I needed three or four drinks.

If I woke up the next morning feeling terrible, it didn't matter. I'd soldier through the day anyway. That was a little trick I picked up in the army. And it was starting to catch up with me.

MILITARY-GRADE DRINKING

One of the best-kept secrets about America's honorable armed service branches is the toxic drinking culture. Many men and women in service, despite being highly trained and highly motivated, have severe drinking problems. I can't tell you how many top-performing, squared-away soldiers I've worked with who executed their duties and responsibilities to the highest of standards, but were actually high-functioning alcoholics. There were too many to count. And before I got out of the army, I took my place among them.

Being in a combat unit, we took physical training (PT) very seriously. We trained hard in order to stay battle ready. The first time I showed up to PT hungover, I was pretty sure I was gonna die. And to be honest, I welcomed the idea. Keeling over and meeting my maker seemed a lot easier than finishing that godforsaken run through the Korean mountains. The only thing that kept me going was knowing that my platoon sergeant wouldn't have let me die even if I tried. He'd have resuscitated me, just so he could roast me in front of the whole unit later. I could just imagine it:

"Yep! Blankenship's ole goat smellin' ass tried to die on the goddamn run this mornin'! I told 'em, if you die out here, I'll prop your stiff ass up at the extra duty desk until you go back to the States! 'Cuz I'm gettin' my time outtcha, one way or the other!"

I didn't want that. So, I kept running.

Each step jostled my whiskey-soaked brain. The entire platoon was in one rhythm, which only amplified the rattle in my head. I plodded along. Seemingly fine on the outside, but hurting bad on the inside.

A lot of us go through life just like that: seemingly fine on the outside, but hurting bad on the inside. If you can relate, understand that you're not alone. We all have our struggles. It's part of the human experience. Sometimes it can feel like we're the only ones hurting while everyone else is living their best lives. That's a well-constructed illusion. It's a mask people wear. And usually, the more picture-perfect someone tries to present themselves, the deeper their issues. As first generation fathers, we don't want the illusion of perfection. We want the strength and insight to see where we're underdeveloped and to improve. So keep running.

When PT was over that morning, I couldn't believe I'd made it. It was a terrible experience, and I swore I would never put myself through that again. By the end of the day, I was laughing about it. Before long, I had another hangover run. Then another one. By the time I got out of the army five years later, not only were they a part of my routine, but my run times were faster than ever.

FINDING MY BALANCE

In the year I took off from drinking, I regained my balance. It felt good to focus my warrior energy on a clearly identified challenge. Because I wasn't drinking in the evenings, I was able to read a lot more, and reinvigorate my intellectual energy. Because I wasn't waking up foggy, I was in a better mood in the mornings. I was more active and got more high-quality time in with the kids.

On the outside, I may not have looked any different. But I could feel a shift inside. I was healthier, happier, and back in my golden zone.

I've taken similar breaks from other things that appeal to my lowest self, just to make sure I stay balanced. I've taken a year off of social media. I've stop gambling altogether. I spent a year consciously avoiding any pornographic or sexualized imagery or content—yep, not one single twerk! I even take focused breaks from swearing—although I don't swear around the kids or listen to anything with swear words around them anyway. These breaks are a way to check myself, to stay in control of my life, and to make sure I'm not falling out of balance—and out of my golden zone.

Listen, I'm not saying you've gotta be a saint. We're all adults. Do what you enjoy doing. But you've got to, GOT TO, keep balanced. If you can't do something in moderation, you can't do it at all. That's just how it's gotta be. Because if your dragon catches you off-balance, it might destroy your life before you're able to center yourself.

At the end of my dry year, I was back in control. I was confident that should my family need me to stop drinking forever, I could. And that's how I feel to this day. I enjoy a drink now—in moderation, and when the time is right. But I'll never let it pull me out of balance again. And more importantly, the self-discovery and healing I've done since that dry year has helped me become more comfortable in the moments of my life, just the way they are. This is the ideal balance we should be seeking to attain in life. Where we're healed, and dragons have no part of us to exploit. Where we can live without fear of becoming addicted to every enjoyable aspect of life. But we have full confidence that should any troubling signs of addiction present themselves, we can find our balance and kill that dragon where it stands.

SUMMARY

Addiction can take all different shapes and forms, but the common denominator is imbalance. The alcoholic, the porn junkie, the emotional eater, the thrice-divorced CEO who works till his family is asleep every night. They're all expressing the same basic imbalance, just in different ways. If they become self-aware, and centered in their three primal energies, they can heal. They can take back power over their lives, and consciously decide the type of person they're going to be. But until they take those steps, their dragons will always be hunting them, and bringing darkness with them.

As first generation fathers, many of us are predisposed to addiction. Some of us are predisposed genetically, others from the scars and traumas we've suffered, others because it was normalized in our environments. Regardless, no one is coming to save us. If we want better for ourselves and for our families, slaying our dragons is our responsibility. You can do it, and you know how. Get balanced, get well, get into your golden zone, and get to swingin' your sword.

GET INTO THE GOLDEN ZONE

Warrior Energy: Slaying dragons means life or death to you and your family. Focus on self-control and discipline. For me, physical exercise and eating healthy keeps me balanced. I also set challenges for myself, such as going certain periods of time without a particular activity, to make sure I can always maintain control over it.

Intellectual Energy: Your best chance at avoiding and overcoming addiction is understanding how it works and why it's happening. The more you know yourself, the more you'll see what's driving your impulses. When people try to fight their addiction with sheer willpower, they almost always lose—because they don't understand what they're truly fighting against. See yourself, face the feelings your dragons use to hunt you, and heal them. That's how you win.

Spiritual Energy: Stay connected to something bigger than yourself. Disconnection and isolation cause an empty aching that dragons hunt. See your body and health as divine gifts that you're charged with maintaining. Helping others and being of service is a great way to find balance in your healthy spiritual energy.

The Golden Zone: Here, you're fully alive. You're not afraid to feel life exactly as it is. You can be in the moment, without needing it to feel different, or better. You're present for the people who need you, and don't let anything, even positive habits or activities, take priority over your loved ones.

The Golden Zone:

- Slay Your Dragons

- Understand Yourself

- Accept Each Moment

CHAPTER 13

● ● ●

ASCENSION: SEEING FROM A HIGHER PERSPECTIVE

Ascension is the act of rising to an important position or a higher level. As a first generation father, you are ascending. You're elevating above negative family patterns. You're ascending beyond the weak and imbalanced versions of yourself, and into your golden zone. You're climbing to all new heights in your thoughts, words, and actions. And the best part is, you're taking your family with you.

In this chapter, I'm going to push the boundaries of our discoveries further. I'm going to reveal to you an advanced way of problem-solving and conflict resolution that pushes your personal growth into hyperdrive. You're balanced in your three primal energies by now. You have access to your full range of masculine and feminine energies as well. You're ready to elevate your perspective, and truly see through the matrix of separation. You're ready for ascension.

MIRROR|MIRROR: SEEING YOURSELF IN OTHERS

One ascended skill that will change your life is the ability to see yourself in others. This, more than anything else I've learned in recent years, has strengthened my relationship with my wife and children. It's helped me grow professionally, too, as I've used it to turn workplace conflicts into win-win resolutions. This ability—to see myself in others—has transformed the way I look at people. Especially people who irritate me. It's turned them—as annoying as I may initially find them—into my own self-awareness tutors. I call this way of seeing Mirror|Mirror, and it goes like this.

When someone bothers me, offends me, or irritates me in some way—I stop, and look for a reflection of *myself* in the other person. Rather than convincing myself that my interpretation of what's happening is "right" and that the other person is "wrong," I look for deeper understanding. I look for a reflection of myself. I look for ways to see how I do the exact same thing that I'm finding so annoying in someone else. And the beautiful part is, if I look with an open heart and an open mind, I almost always find it. This is true whether the person irritating me is my wife, my kids, or a total stranger.

Mirror|Mirror: what I see in you is a reflection of me. What you see in others, is a reflection of you.

This ideology isn't new. History's most profound spiritual teachers have long expressed variations of the idea that life shows us versions of ourselves through others. One of psychology's most revered psychoanalysts, Carl Jung, once said:

"Everything that irritates us in others, can lead to an understanding of ourselves."

After years of thinking such ideas were just philosophical fluff, I've finally arrived at an understanding that has practical purposes in my daily life as a husband and father. Everything connects. Now, Mirror|Mirror is a tool that I use to turn conflict and tense situations into divine messengers that help me grow. I'm now thankful for our family conflicts when they arise, because I know how to turn them into gold. Here's a quick, real-life example.

A few years back, Adrian went through a spell where he refused to do his homework. He was a smart kid, and his grades were great. He loved reading on his own and thinking about issues that most kids his age would find too much like school.

But when it came time to do homework, he'd just sit there. When Sarah and I would ask him what his problem was, he had all sorts of excuses.

"I'm not sure what to do."

"I don't know what to write."

"I don't understand the question."

None of these excuses made any sense, though. Sarah and I would sit next to him and go over the material. As he explained the assignment, it was obvious he understood the subject matter plenty well enough to do the work. But when it came time for him to write down the answer—the answer he just said to us out loud—nothin'. He sat there, staring at the blank page.

No, he doesn't have any type of learning disabilities, dyslexia, vision difficulty, etc. No, we weren't putting undue pressure on him, or being overly critical of his work. Honestly, Sarah and I don't put a ton of stock into homework. We just needed the kid to freakin' jot somthin' down so we could all move on with our lives! It was a very frustrating phase. My initial feeling, as you may have guessed, was disrespect. But I'd healed that wound and was able to look at this problem from a different angle. When I looked at it through the filter of Mirror|Mirror, I was shocked at what I discovered.

For years before that, I'd been saying I was going to write a book. I felt I had some great ideas that could be of help to people. When talking about my unwritten book, I understood the subject matter at a high level, and I had lots of creative ideas. But when it was time to write—for me to do my homework—I just sat there. Staring at the blank page.

"I'm not sure what to do."

"I don't know what to write."

"I don't understand the question."

Because I was balanced in my golden zone, I was able to look at Adrian's refusal to do the work he was clearly capable of doing as a divine lesson for me. As a reflection of myself. That changed everything. I became thankful for the whole experience! I became appreciative that he wasn't doing his work. He helped me see I needed to fix myself before I could correct him.

With this new understanding, I started my book in earnest—this book. I stopped overthinking, stopped bullshitting myself with lame excuses, and got to it. Because I was now looking at his stubbornness against his homework as a gift, my attitude toward him softened. That little softening on my part allowed him to relax a bit. I stopped overthinking, he stopped overthinking. I worked, he worked. I was supportive of every small step he made to get out of his own way, and he's since totally outgrown his homework hang-up. That little conflict only made our relationship stronger and brought us closer together. Since then, *First Generation Father* has been written and published, and Adrian is an honor student with no homework hang-ups. Everything connects.

Not only does Mirror|Mirror reveal parts of you that need work during interpersonal conflicts, but the principles apply to situations or circumstances too.

Here are some quick examples on how you can look at stressful situations in a way that benefits you:

Old Perspective: Ugh! I just cleaned up and here comes my spouse makin' a mess.

Mirror|Mirror Perspective: What are some ways I can be more supportive of my partner's efforts both around the house and in our relationship?

Old Perspective: My boss sucks.

Mirror|Mirror Perspective: How am I not doing the best job I can for the people I'm responsible for leading? Are there aspects of my life I'm not "managing" well?

Old Perspective: Someone's tone of voice bothers you.

Mirror|Mirror Perspective: Does my tone ever come off as rude or bothersome? I'm gonna be more conscious of the way I speak to people.

There are countless opportunities to see yourself in others. The more you develop your technique, the more you advance your personal growth—and your ability to effectively lead your family—to the next level. However, there's something you need to be on the lookout for. An obstacle that comes from within that doesn't necessarily want to see you grow.

THE EGO'S RESISTANCE

When you first hear this Mirror|Mirror concept, it might make you feel uncomfortable. Part of you may even think, *that's bullshit*. The part of you thinking that is your ego. As a wise T-shirt once read, *your ego is not your amigo.*

Many philosophers and psychologists have dedicated their entire lives to studying, interpreting, and defining the ego. To me, the ego simply means a sense of separation from others. It's *me* centered. I, me, mine, my; how often someone uses these self-focused words will let you know very quickly if they're operating from their ego.

Of course, we do need some ego. A little ego is good for our healthy individuality and our personal pride. But the ego is gluttonous, it always wants more of us. It doesn't want to be a balanced, healthy part of you. It wants to take you over. And if you don't check it, it will.

The unhealthy ego keeps you from ascending. Since the ego is separation, it keeps you from seeing yourself in others. It whispers in your ear that you're right, and others are wrong. It keeps you blind to your own glaring flaws. It will convince you that you're great, while simultaneously preventing you from ascending to actual greatness.

Your ego does much worse than just sit in the road, blocking your path to ascension. It actively works to keep you from growing. It intentionally sabotages your personal development. Why? Because our egos are weak. They're fragile. And they know that as we ascend and evolve personally—as we wake up to just how powerful and capable we are—our egos lose power over us. And they don't want that.

Unhealthy egos can only live in shallow and dark energies. The light and clean air of ascension kills it, and restores balance. As first generation fathers, overcoming our unhealthy egos is a make-or-break task for our relationships, and for our families. Understanding that there are parts of yourself actively working against your own growth—then overcoming those lower parts of yourself—is a metamorphosis we've all got to go through. It's part of ascending. Deep down, you've always known this. You've felt it, even if you weren't sure how to say it. You knew part of you felt splintered, broken apart. Not quite whole and well. That's your ego working against you.

When you're exposed to trauma and conflict, it's natural to want to protect yourself. For a lot of us, our protection came in the form of thick, unhealthy egos. At the time, they were necessary! Mine kept me feeling a sense of self-worth when the world would have convinced me I was worthless. In your own way, your heavy ego has served you too. You needed it to survive. And you *did* survive!

Now, it's time to evolve past surviving and ascend into thriving. The armor of ego has protected you up to this point on your journey, but it's too heavy to carry up the rest of the mountain. It doesn't serve you anymore. You've got to set it down, and walk the rest of the way protected by your balance. Set down your separation, your defensiveness, and your fear...and ascend to your highest self. This is what your family needs from you. It's what you're here for.

How do you set down your ego? You already know the answer: balance. Focus your warrior energy on shining the light of awareness on the darkest parts of yourself. Focus your intellectual energy on rewriting your mental script—the underlying thoughts constantly narrating your life in your head. Don't let them autoplay—that tends to be ego. Consciously choose your thoughts, and reinforce them over and over until they become the new underlying script. Keep your spiritual energy bucket full of appreciation and purpose. This will help you feel your way through the illusion of separation and stay connected to life itself. Stay positive, stay thankful, and stay topped off.

The ability to see yourself in others is pivotal to your ascension. If you don't master it, you'll miss out on critical learning opportunities. Life, however, doesn't allow us to advance while there are still unlearned lessons right in front of us. Instead, we find ourselves repeating situations, experiences, even the type of people we meet, over and over, until we make the connection, and learn what we're supposed to learn. Once you do, you can level up. But not before. What I'm saying is, we *will* learn. We have no choice. The only question is how much pain do we force ourselves to experience first?

THE UMBRELLA OF TRANSGRESSION

In order to see ourselves in others, we've got to look from a higher place. The higher you ascend, the more you can see. While sitting in a car, it can be hard to see how the road you're on connects to an adjoining road. From an airplane, you can see how a whole city connects.

From an ascended perspective, we understand how one character flaw can be expressed in many different ways. Similar to how allergies may cause a stuffy nose in one person, a headache in another, and a cough in another. They all have the same root problem, but express it differently. The character flaws we see through Mirror|Mirror work this same way.

Here's an example.

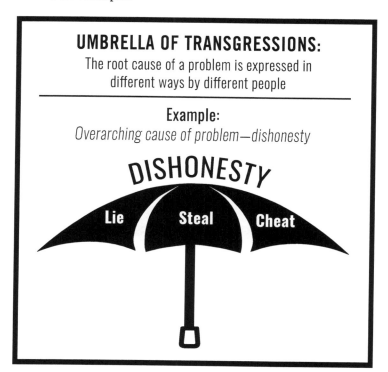

UMBRELLA OF TRANSGRESSIONS:
The root cause of a problem is expressed in different ways by different people

Example:
Overarching cause of problem—dishonesty

DISHONESTY

Lie   Steal   Cheat

In this case, the connection was dishonesty. Now, how foolish would the cheater be to think himself better than the thief? Or the liar? In order to best see yourself in others, you must have the wisdom to see through the superficiality of the transgressions—and to understand the overarching umbrella that connects them.

Sometimes, acts under the same umbrella of transgression can even look totally opposite of each other. But under the surface, they're driven by the same flaws. Here's an example of how that happens in unhealthy relationships.

OVERARCHING TRANSGRESSION: SELFISHNESS

He strings her along in a relationship he isn't fully committed to, knowing it won't last.

She tries to trap him by getting pregnant with a baby she knows he doesn't want.

While both of these actions look different on the surface—he's noncommittal, she's pregnant—they fall under the same umbrella—selfishness. He doesn't care about what she wants, and she doesn't care about what he wants. If they were wise, they'd be able to see themselves in each other's flaws and grow. But if they're driven by ego and the illusion that they are right while the other person is wrong, they'll continue to point fingers, justify their own behavior, and miss significant opportunities for growth.

Use your ascended perspective to see more clearly and to make big-picture connections. When you find your attention drawn to particular flaws of a person, stop. Find your balance.

Check your ego, and look to see yourself. Master this, and your spouse's annoying traits will become an asset for *your* personal growth. Teaching your children will lead to your own learning. Lead becomes gold. And everything becomes your teacher.

PAIN AS ROCKET FUEL

Speaking of ascension, have you ever seen a space shuttle launch? It's a stunning combination of balance, power, and ingenuity. For a launch to be successful, it requires its own sort of golden zone balance. And with each launch, there's a very real possibility of catastrophic failure.

The shuttle itself is a work of art. It's sleek and aerodynamic, despite being enormous in size (which is its own beautiful duality). It stands on the launchpad, tall and proud, staring at the heavens. Ready to ascend.

In seconds, incomprehensible amounts of force will be battling for the shuttle's destiny. Rockets pushing it up, gravity pulling it down. It's a pivotal moment. Fly or die. As a first generation father, you're facing this very situation in your own life. You're the shuttle. The gravity pulling you downward is your past, your scars, your pain. The heaven ahead of you is your ascended self and a healthy and happy home for your family to thrive in. So what's it gonna be, fly or die?

3...2...1...Massive plumes of smoke and fire pour out from under the shuttle. It shakes as the opposing energies wrestle. Slowly, it inches upward. But gravity is resilient. The future hangs in the balance. Every day there are elements from your past trying to pull you back, pull you down, and end your mission in catastrophic failure. But your mission isn't just yours. Your family is on board. Your future is on board. If you fail to launch, they all go down with you.

Real space shuttles have a special resource they use to help them launch. They're boosters, attached to the sides of the shuttle, and they're filled with a special fuel to give them an extra push. In order for you to fly, you've got to take any negative feelings you may have—any pain, resentment, confusion, or frustration—and use it as fuel to help you launch. If you harness that power, it can provide the additional thrust—motivation—you need to escape the pull of what's behind you, and soar.

GROW ANYWAY

As you ascend and elevate through various levels of life, you'll naturally experience some changes. The things you'll find yourself drawn to, and wanting to focus your time and energy on, will change too.

As you evolve out of the ego state, and past the illusion of separation, you'll no longer want to judge others. You'll feel uncomfortable and wrong talking about people, or being around others who are. You'll have ascended past gossip and pettiness. You'll be high vibin', and won't have any room in your golden zone for unhealthy energies.

This growth sounds great, and it is. But still, it may strain some relationships in your life. Not everybody is going to like your new position. Some people—even people who love you—will want you to keep the same perspectives you've always had. For their own imbalanced reasons, they don't want you to grow. That can't matter. Keep growing anyway.

Your family needs you to ascend. To best serve them now—and as the people they are on their way to becoming—you've got to keep evolving. If that means certain friends or extended family play a less significant role in your life for a while—that's just how it has to be. They can grow with you or watch from a distance. But you can't stop, and you certainly can't go backward.

Trying to explain your heightened view to a person stuck on the ground level doesn't work. They'll misunderstand you. They'll take offense to your perspective—misinterpreting your desire for growth as an insult to them. They'll project their own character flaws and limited understandings onto you. Don't waste your time. Ascension can only happen when a person seeks it out for themselves. So, instead of trying to explain to others how to level up, you just keep doing it, and let them watch. You ascend, you evolve, you lead from the front. Your growth might just be the motivation others need to start their own ascension.

GET INTO THE GOLDEN ZONE

Warrior Energy: Overcome your ego. Stay balanced, and look for yourself in the flaws of others. Starve out low-level energies such as judging, gossip, jealousy, and pettiness. Being a leader will require you to walk long stretches of this road alone. Persist.

Intellectual Energy: Seeing from this heightened perspective can feel scary. Don't let the initial unfamiliarity of it cause you to revert back to your lower self. Practice your new way of seeing often, reinforcing the pattern in your mind. Your newly acquired skills are powerful. Only use them to help people, never to hurt, exploit, or manipulate. No matter what happens, stay balanced, and look for the lesson. Everything is your teacher.

Spiritual Energy: The wiser you become, the more you understand that your wisdom isn't yours. It's being provided to you, for you, through you. We all have the same access to this universal wisdom. Accessing it is just a matter of staying spiritually energized, and keeping our egos from blocking the signal. Staying connected here will open you up to profound ways of being of service to your family.

The Golden Zone: Here, you've unlocked new, ascended insight and understanding. This changes the dynamics of your family. Every conflict has the potential to be a win-win situation, leaving both parties wiser and more evolved on the other side of it.

Parents are leading by example and teaching their children these ascended life skills. Children are unintentionally teaching their parents, helping them evolve by reflecting back to them their own character flaws under the umbrella of transgression. You see divinity in others and feel it in yourself.

CHAPTER 14

• • •

CONCLUSION: FORGIVENESS

Our plane hit a patch of turbulence, and I looked over to make sure Adrian was OK.

He smiled and gave me a thumbs-up. It had been over sixteen years since I last saw my dad. Now, I was flying back to Ohio to get some closure with him. And I brought my son with me.

I wasn't sure what to expect from the meeting, but I knew it needed to happen. In the years since I'd last seen him, so much had changed in my life. I'd become a man. I'd gotten married, become a father myself, and healed from all the trauma and drama I grew up around. At least, I thought I'd healed. That's really why I wanted to visit him—to make sure. I needed to look him in his eyes in his own home, and make sure I wasn't harboring any resentment in my heart. And I wanted my son to watch me do it. I felt this was the last step in truly breaking the cycle of family dysfunction. The last time I'd seen my dad before this visit, he was in prison.

One day, when I was in high school, my mom showed me a newspaper article. She chewed at her lip while I read it. It was from the *Toledo Blade*, the same newspaper I'd delivered as a kid. It was a write-up about a man who'd been arrested for severely assaulting a woman. The details were foggy. But two things were clear: the woman was seriously injured, and the man who hurt her was my dad.

When it was all said and done, a judge sentenced him to ten years in state prison. I'm still not exactly sure what happened on the night in question, nor am I curious to know. I'm too focused on escaping the gravitational pull of what's behind me to look back. What I can say for sure is, after all the pain he'd caused others over the years, I wasn't surprised he eventually wound up behind bars. Despite the fact that he and I were never particularly close, he asked me to come visit him while he was serving his time.

Going to a prison—even just to visit—is a surreal experience. This one sat in a big open field in rural Ohio. As I drove the main road toward it, it sat on the horizon like a dense brick. As I got closer, and it came more into view, it looked squatty. Heavy, somehow. As if the building itself was chained to the ground. In the parking lot, I got that old familiar lump in my throat. I felt nervous, I felt unsafe, I felt normal.

As a young man, there's a swirling mix of confusing emotions when your dad is in prison. Part of you feels doomed to the same fate. Part of you feels embarrassed. Part of you feels resentful. Part of you feels judged by others. Part of you feels proud—*see, we don't give a fuck!* Not giving a fuck is as good as currency in some environments. I was in high school, still a young man and very much at risk myself. My future undecided, spinning in the air like a flipped coin. Heads or tails. Build or destroy. Lead or gold.

Layered rows of razor wire decorated all the fence tops. They glistened in the sun, surrounding the entire perimeter of the building. They looked like a beautiful trap. Teasing the inmates, dangling freedom just on the other side of their gnarled metal teeth.

Inside the building, the atmosphere was oppressive. The yellow lights buzzed. The air felt thick and stale. Guards gave me distrusting glances as they checked me through security. Visiting someone in prison, you leave your assumption of innocence at the gate.

The visiting area was a large, open gymnasium. As I waited for my dad to come down, I couldn't help but look at the other inmates. I found myself wondering, *What are their stories? How did they wind up here?* Today, I would phrase it, *What obstacles in their lives were they unable to transform into gold? How are their three primal energies off-balance? What malformations have they suffered?*

I'm not some bleeding heart. I understand that we all have to be accountable for our actions. I feel I understand that more than most. But I also know that everything connects. When I saw these men in prison—or when I think about all the fathers, brothers, sons, daughters, and mothers locked up all across this country—rather than passing judgment on them, I look to see myself. And I'm reminded of the biblical proverb, "There, but for the grace of God, go I."

Whenever our visits were over and I'd leave the prison, I would always feel terrible. Not only was I emotionally drained, but the energy of the place would stick to me. It felt as if I were aligning myself with it, somehow calling it into my own existence. On my last visit, I hooked my dad up with all the soda and microwavable chicken wings he wanted from the vending machine. Said my goodbyes. Walked past the gnashing razor wire—and vowed never to return. That was the last time I'd seen him.

The pilot announced that we'd be landing soon. And now, sixteen years later, I was about to make sure that I'd really mastered the final step in being a first generation father: forgiveness.

THE POWER OF FORGIVENESS

In the last chapter we talked about ascension, which means climbing to the highest version of yourself. One mandatory stop we've all got to make along that path is forgiveness. This is nonnegotiable. If you're going to level up, and lead your family from a balanced place of pure love, you've got to master forgiveness.

I've shared a lot of personal scars with you throughout this book. I've laid myself open. And I did it because I need you to believe me when I tell you this: to fully break the cycle you came from, to completely heal both mentally and emotionally, you've got to forgive those who have hurt you. You have to. Forgiveness is the last step in healing and moving forward.

When someone has hurt you, violated your trust, or put you through painful experiences, forgiving them is hard. It can feel wrong, like letting the guilty party off the hook. But here's a secret about forgiveness:

> You don't forgive someone for the peace it brings them, you forgive them for the peace it brings you.

In the years it took me to write this book, I had lots of deeply personal conversations with people. When I explained my idea of first generation father, many folks opened up to me about their own childhood (and adult) traumas. I'm humbled and moved whenever someone trusts me enough to share their vulnerability with me. More than once, someone's told me something personal and then admitted, *I've never told that to anyone before.* Some of the things I've heard were flat-out heartbreaking.

So many people—regular-looking people—both men and women, have suffered unimaginable traumas and hardships. Often as children, and often at the hands of adults who were supposed to be protecting them. Some of the stories I heard brought me right back to being a scared and confused kid myself. But when I would ask these good people, who had overcome such fucked-up situations, how they managed to beat their past, I learned that we'd all used the same tool—forgiveness.

Forgiving isn't easy, but it's the only way to keep your past from hurting you now. You may very well have legitimate reasons to be angry, bitter, and disappointed. But I promise you, holding onto those negative emotions won't punish the person who wronged you. It punishes *you*, and it punishes your family because you can't give them the best version of you when you're hanging on to hate.

WHAT FORGIVENESS ISN'T

Forgiving someone doesn't mean acting like nothing ever happened. Nor does it mean you have to give this person access to your life or to your family. It doesn't mean you have to trust a person, or let them occupy a position from where they may hurt you again. Denying reality and letting someone hurt you or your family (again) because you forgave them isn't forgiveness, it's foolishness.

To forgive simply means to stop being at odds with the painful thing that has *already* happened. When you forgive, you stop thinking things should have gone differently than they did. You let go and stop replaying painful scenarios in your head over and over. Forgiving strips the past from its power over your future. We all have scars. But our past has already hurt us. We can't let it keep hurting us. Forgive and set yourself free.

NEXT-LEVEL FORGIVENESS

The highest level of forgiveness you can ascend to is to forgive those who aren't sorry. By comparison, it's easy to forgive someone who admits they were wrong, owns up to it, and apologizes. But situations rarely work out that neat and clean, especially in family drama. Sometimes the person who owes you a big apology is too small to give it to you. Or too off-balance to even see how their actions affected you. Sometimes we're hurt by narcissists who, lacking empathy and self-awareness, are far more likely to rewrite history, making themselves the victim, than to apologize. These people are often family members. Which makes a tough situation even tougher.

This is some seriously heavy lead, and it's gonna take all of your warrior, intellectual, and spiritual energy to transform it into gold. But you can do it. You have the skills and the understanding to make it happen. Plus, you realize what's at stake for you and your family if you don't. You've come all this way, finish the journey. Evolve. Ascend. Forgive.

FORGIVING YOURSELF

One important, often overlooked, aspect of forgiveness is learning to forgive yourself. You can't ascend if you're still punishing yourself for past mistakes or holding grudges against yourself. As people mature emotionally and spiritually, I've seen some fall into the trap of graciously forgiving others for their mistakes and shortcomings, then relentlessly beating themselves up for their own.

Judging yourself harshly is one sneaky way your ego tries to maintain control over you. Mine still tries to manipulate me in this way. When I make a mistake, I recognize where I'm wrong, and work hard to improve and move forward. But sometimes my ego won't let me. It wants to keep reminding me about my flaws and imperfections. If you've ever been caught in the mental loop of replaying a mistake you've made over and over in your head, you know what psychological torture that can be.

Listen, healthy accountability for your actions is great. It's honorable. But it's the unhealthy ego that takes the idea of accountability and weaponizes it against us. Trapping us in a mental maze of regret, self-blame, and unhappiness.

I've got bad news for you: you haven't made your last mistake. Neither have I. Neither have the people we love. We're human. Screwing up is how we learn! We make bad decisions, reflect on them, and come out better for it on the other side. You cannot ascend if you're continually hammering yourself. Take the lessons your mistakes brought to light, and bring them with you into a new day. You can't grow into a better, highly evolved version of yourself without getting some things wrong along the way. So be kind to yourself. You're never gonna be perfect. Take responsibility where it's due, feel appreciative for the opportunity to grow, shore up your faults, and forgive yourself.

CLOSING THE LOOP

Our plane landed safely. Adrian and I picked up our luggage and exited the airport in our rental car with zero hassles and in record time. I took this as a good sign. As we drove, we laughed and joked about what the upcoming experience might be like. And how foreign a concept it was for Adrian to imagine being in my situation.

I'd forgiven my dad. I had no hard feelings lurking. I had long since turned any old pains into rocket fuel, and I was free from the gravity of my past. I had learned to turn lead into gold. My less than ideal upbringing had been exactly what I needed to turn me into the best husband and father I could be. Not perfect, but good, and still improving. When I pulled up to his apartment, I sat in the car for a minute. Trying to examine my deepest feelings. I was checking to see if I felt nervous, or scared, or uneasy. But I didn't feel any of that. I felt normal. My new normal. Which is healthy, happy, and balanced.

I chose to bring Adrian for several reasons. I thought it would be good for a young male to see his father working through forgiveness, and processing potentially complex emotions. He's always been highly intelligent. And I felt he could handle the experience. I told him exactly why I was going, and why I wanted him to come. He understood, and agreed it was a good idea.

However, I did not think it would be a good idea to bring Sarah or Cassidy. The last thing I wanted to do was expose my wife and daughter to any bullshit. I wasn't sure how the visit was gonna go. There were a lot of ways for it to potentially jump off the tracks. Rather than risk that, I left them home. To this day, neither of them have ever met my father.

Another reason I brought Adrian is so that he could see and understand that his biological grandfather is a Black man. Although Adrian is one-quarter Black, you wouldn't know it by looking at him. Sarah was born in England and moved to the U.S. as a child. I'm mixed, and my father is very dark-skinned. So my kids have a pretty unique range of racial and cultural diversity in their blood. Given America's long and complicated history with race, I felt it especially important for my son to understand all of his makeup.

The trip went great. Adrian got to meet my father and also lots of other family members for the first time. He met my aunts, uncles, cousins, and their children. He met some of my brothers and sisters who have different mothers than me, and their children. He met my father's mother! He met as many people as I could stick him in front of—Black, White, and every beautiful shade in between. It was amazing to see him being loved and welcomed by such a diverse group of people that were all family. That alone was worth the trip.

While I was there, my dad apologized. For everything. When he started, I almost stopped him. I had already confirmed what I came to confirm. I was sure that I'd already truly forgiven him. However, I understood that he needed this apology for his own closure. Similar to how forgiving others can make us feel complete, apologizing when we need to has the same effect. To continue on his path to healing, and ascending, I knew he needed to apologize. So, I sat quietly, and let him.

Afterward, the three of us went out to a nice dinner. Where we ate, talked, and laughed. When I left to go home, I assured him that he and I were good. And we are. That trip was the last time I saw him.

Years have passed since then, and that's OK. Remember, forgiving doesn't have to mean giving someone full access to you. And it certainly doesn't mean giving them access to your partner, children, or the people in this world you're charged with protecting and safeguarding. But I don't have any bitterness in my heart toward him, or my mother, or her boyfriends, or my grandfather, or the kid who pushed me down and stole my paper route money. I understand now that the only reason anyone ever hurts anyone else is they are off-balance themselves. Not quite able to get into their golden zones and stay there. I'm proud of anyone making an effort to improve and be better. Because, really, that's all any of us can do.

WALK YOUR PATH

The mission you're on—to become a fully healed, self-actualized, balanced leader for your family—is the most noble mission any man can go on. I commend your efforts. Thank you so much for taking the time to read *First Generation Father*. I hope it helps you find your golden zone and complete your mission.

The impact of what you're doing may be deeper than you realize. It's not just your partners and children who benefit from your growth. It's your sisters, and brothers, and cousins, and nieces, and nephews. It's people who you might not even realize are watching you, looking to you for leadership, but they are. They're looking for you to provide examples on how to build positive, loving relationships, and strong families. So many people are looking for somebody, anybody, to show them that healthy and happy homes are not just the stuff of fairy tales. I nominate you.

You and I are in a unique position. We have the ability to be a blessing both forward and backward. Our growth frees our children from having to suffer the same scars we did, that's the blessing forward. Our success redeems our parents for mistakes they made when they were off-balance themselves, that's the blessing backward. Our forgiveness, healing, and ascension generate a light that shines on everyone we meet. As we find our golden zones—and build a life there—we set an example for others to follow. Everything connects.

Remember, facing your scars and learning to acknowledge how they've affected you is the start to being a fully healed first generation father. This means tuning into what you're feeling, and being aware of what's truly driving your actions. Once you start to see yourself clearly, identify where you're out of balance in your warrior, intellectual, or spiritual energies, and adjust from there.

What you look for determines what you see. I see fortuitous synchronicities and opportunities to be thankful everywhere, because that's what I look for. Practice doing this, and even obstacles and challenges eventually reveal themselves as just the gold you needed. Your stress will decrease. You'll feel good physically, mentally, spiritually, and emotionally. Your relationships will be stronger and more meaningful than ever. Your finances will evolve from surviving to thriving, and you'll find deep satisfaction in looking for ways to give your talents to the world. You'll be in the golden zone, where you're not only changing life for your family, but you're planting seeds that will benefit those you love for generations to come.

You've said you'd do anything for your family. Now is your time to prove it. In order to become the man they need you to be, you're gonna have to fight your ass off. You need full access to healthy warrior energy to overcome your lower self, defeat your ego, and persist against the discomfort and pain of growth. You must fight, and you must win. Your family depends on it.

The understanding you've discovered recently should cause you to look at the world—and yourself—differently. It may feel like you're waking up from a long sleep. It may even feel like you're waking up for the first time ever. That's normal. But you should know, there is no going back to sleep now. There's no snooze button on the level of awareness you've just ascended to. From here on out, you are fully responsible for every choice you make in your life. There are no more subconscious, unhealed wounds driving your actions. You have all the understanding required to move into your fullest, most powerful, creative self. You know everything you need to know. You're about to move into the most deeply satisfying years of your life as a spouse, as a parent, and as a person. You're ready.

Your understanding—your peace—exists at a level deeper than thought. It exists in your soul, in your spirit. Internalize your understanding, and let it reveal to you the divine correlation between all things. Find your purpose and stay connected to it. When all else fails, serve others.

As you ascend to the highest levels of your personal growth, and your spiritual bucket stays full, you'll take no pride in judging. You'll see yourself in other people's flaws. In doing so, you'll grow stronger as a person, while also strengthening your ability to see the divine connection among all people. You'll know, in the deepest parts of yourself, that everything connects.

Apply these teachings and practices in your life, and you'll be the unstoppable force of love and leadership that your family and community needs from you. There will be no limit to how far your influence will reach, to how much you can accomplish, or to how much love, happiness, and success will be granted to your family. The journey never ends. There is no arriving. Only being in the golden zone in this current moment. And this current moment. And this current moment. For all the moments we can.

ABOUT THE AUTHOR

ANTHONY BLANKENSHIP was born to an unwed, teen-age mother and a father who would later serve time in prison. His home life exposed him to violence, drugs, and poverty at a young age. At fifteen, struggling with unhealed mental and emotional wounds, Anthony committed a crime that nearly cost him his life.

He used this low point to slingshot himself forward, focusing on growth, accountability, and evolution. Anthony searched for ways to educate himself and break free from the cyclical pull of his early environment. Today, the former army officer has found his golden zone. A happily married father of two, he has developed a philosophy that allowed him to heal and lead his family into health, happiness, and prosperity. Now, he's ready to share this philosophy with the world.

For information on how you can donate a copy of *First Generation Father* to readers in need, visit AnthonyBlankenship.com.

Printed in Great Britain
by Amazon